D0354962

FUTURE
English for Results

5

WORKBOOK

Kathryn L. O'Dell

Janet Gokay

Series Consultants

Beatriz B. Díaz

Ronna Magy

Federico Salas-Isnardi

PEARSON
Longman

Future 5
English for Results
Workbook

Copyright © 2010 by Pearson Education, Inc.
All rights reserved.
No part of this publication may be reproduced, stored in a retrieval system, or transmitted in any form or by any means, electronic, mechanical, photocopying, recording, or otherwise, without the prior permission of the publisher.

Pearson Education, 10 Bank Street, White Plains, NY 10606

Staff credits: The people who made up the *Future 5 Workbook* team, representing editorial, production, design, and manufacturing are Elizabeth Carlson, Aerin Csigay, Dave Dickey, Nancy Flaggman, Irene Frankel, Michael Kemper, Niki Lee, Rebecca Ortman, Liza Pleva, Stella Reilly, Barbara Sabella, and Kim Steiner.

Cover design: Rhea Banker
Cover photo: Kathy Lamm/Getty Images
Text design: Barbara Sabella
Text composition: Rainbow Graphics
Text font: 13 pt Minion

Illustration credits: Pages 90, 114 Kenneth Batelman; **56** Stephen Hutchings; **50** Steve Schulman; **32, 38** Gary Torrisi; **73, 74** Meryl Treatner
Photo credits: Page 2 (A) Fotolia.com, (B) Shutterstock, (C) Shutterstock, (D) Shutterstock; **6** Courtesy of Kathryn L. O'Dell; **10** Shutterstock; **15** Shutterstock; **22** Corbis Premium RF/Alamy; **27** Shutterstock; **31** Shutterstock; **38** Rubberball/Jupiterimages; **60** Bob Daemmrich/PhotoEdit; **69** Shutterstock; **76** Shutterstock; **77** ImageState/Alamy; **78** Jeff Greenberg/Alamy; **82** Rischgitz/Getty Images; **84** Jeff Greenberg/Alamy; **88** Michael Dwyer/Alamy; **96** (top) Library of Congress, (bottom) Michael Ventura/Alamy; **100** Black Star/Alamy; **108-109** Shutterstock; **114** Juraj Kovacik/Dreamstime.com; **122** Shutterstock; **124** Warner Bros./Photofest.

ISBN-13: 978-0-13-240922-3
ISBN-10: 0-13-240922-4

Printed in the United States of America
5 6 7 8 9 10—V011—18 17 16 15 14 13

Contents

To the Teacher

The *Future 5 Workbook* complements what students have learned in the Student Book. Each workbook unit follows the lesson order of the Student Book and provides supplemental practice in grammar, life skills, reading, writing, and vocabulary. Students can complete the workbook exercises outside the classroom as homework or during class time to extend instruction.

UNIT STRUCTURE

Grammar

Grammar exercises include sentence completion, sentence writing, sentence scrambles, matching, and multiple choice. Exercises progress from very controlled to open and provide ample written practice with the target structure. Exercises are contextualized, recycling themes and vocabulary from the unit, so that grammar practice is authentic and meaningful.

Life Skills

Practice focuses on functional language, practical skills, and authentic printed materials such as driving directions, technical diagrams, and maps. Each Life Skill lesson also includes a Study Skill exercise. Study Skill exercises build students' abilities to interpret information presented in different types of charts and graphs.

Reading

Each reading page includes a new, high-interest, informative article related to the theme of the Student Book unit. Reading Skills presented in the Student Book, such as finding the main idea, are reviewed and practiced through pre-reading or comprehension tasks.

Dictionary Skills and Word Study

Each unit includes a Dictionary Skills and Word Study lesson. The Dictionary Skill exercises feature excerpts from the *Longman Dictionary of American English* and present and practice integral dictionary skills such as identifying parts of speech and recognizing multiple meanings of an entry. The Word Study exercise provides and practices skills such as identifying suffixes and prefixes.

Writing

The writing page focuses on editing. The lesson begins with a paragraph that a student might have written. Students edit the paragraph according to the writing tip presented in the Student Book. For example, students may be asked to delete unnecessary information from a paragraph. In addition, the lesson often involves an error-correction exercise, giving students practice in proofreading.

Vocabulary

Each workbook unit culminates with a vocabulary lesson that reviews and expands on the vocabulary presented in the Student Book. Each vocabulary lesson includes a learning strategy tip that supports persistence by giving students ideas for continued learning outside the classroom and can be used with any new words students encounter.

ANSWER KEY

Answers to all exercises are found in the back of the Workbook.

ORIENTATION

Before students use the Workbook for the first time, direct them to the orientation material on the next page. Go through the questions with the class. Answer any questions students may have so they can get the most out of using the Workbook.

To the Student

LEARN ABOUT YOUR BOOK

A PAIRS. Look at Unit 1. Write the subject of each lesson on the line. Use choices from the box. Some subjects will be used more than once.

> Grammar   Life Skills and Study Skills   Reading
> Vocabulary   Writing   Dictionary Skills and Word Study

Lesson 1: _____

Lesson 2: _____

Lesson 3 & 4: _____

Lessons 5: _____

Lesson 6: _____

Expansion: _____

Lessons 7, 8, & 9: _____

Review & Expand: _____

B PAIRS. Look again at Unit 1. Find the pages with the following information or activities. Write the page number(s) on the line.

1. advice to help you become a better reader ____

2. practice reading and understanding statistics ____

3. practice to help you improve your writing skills ____

4. advice to help you learn new vocabulary ____

C PAIRS. Look at pages 12 & 13. What specific skills are practiced in this Dictionary Skills and Word Study Lesson?

_____

D PAIRS. Look at page 130. Answer the questions.

1. What information is on this page? _____

2. Find *Answers will vary. Possible answers include:* What does *Answers will vary* mean?

_____

Lesson 1: Life Skills and Study Skills

LIFE SKILLS

Read the job ads. Then read about the interests and abilities of four people. Which jobs should they apply for? Write the jobs under the pictures.

Medical office assistant	Security guard	PT installation technician trainee	STORE MANAGER
Requirements: Excellent telephone skills on busy, multi-line system Ability to work under pressure Outstanding organization 2 years of medical office experience preferred	Security service company seeks responsible, punctual security guards *Requirements:* · Reliable transportation · Integrity and honesty · Excellent communication skills	Proficiency troubleshooting hardware and software technical issues in PC/LAN networking environment Job requires physical labor, servicing IP cameras 24 feet off the ground. Must not have fear of heights.	High energy, team player **Requirements:** Able to manage store operations effectively Retail experience Positive attitude

Hi, My name is Galina. I'm bilingual in English and Russian and I enjoy working with people. I have retail experience and some experience as an assistant manager.

Hi, I'm Serge. I take pride in my work and I'm honest and reliable. I have experience as a school crossing guard and driver. I'm also a volunteer policeman in my community.

_____

Hello, my name is Thai Dang. I'm good at solving problems and I enjoy working with my hands. I like computers and communications technology.

Hi, I'm Vera. My background is in office work. I can manage time well, and I'm good with phone systems and computers. I would like to work in the health care field.

_____

STUDY SKILL: Understand statistics

Look at the chart from the U.S. Department of Labor. Complete the sentences.

Occupation	Employment number (numbers in thousands)		Change		Earnings*
	2006	2016	Numeric (in thousands)	Percent	
registered nurses	2,505	3,092	587	23.5	VH
office clerks	3,200	3,604	404	12.6	L
bookkeeping, accounting, and auditing clerks	2,114	2,337	264	12.5	L
executive secretaries and administrative assistants	1,618	1,857	239	14.8	H
computer software engineers	507	733	226	44.6	VH
accountants and auditors	1,274	1,500	226	17.7	VH
truck drivers	1,860	2,053	193	10.4	H
medical assistants	417	565	148	35.4	L
computer systems analysts	504	650	146	29	VH
teacher assistants	1,312	1,449	137	10.4	VL

Occupational Employment Statistics

*Earnings: VH = very high ($46,300 or more)   H = high ($30,630 to $46,300)   L = low ($21,260 to $30,560)
VL = very low (up to $21,220)

Source: U.S. Bureau of Labor Statistics

1. The occupation showing the fastest job growth is _____.

2. Between 2006 and 2016, office clerk jobs will grow by _____ percent.

3. In 2006, there were _____ bookkeeping, accounting, and auditing clerks.

4. By 2016, the number of medical assistants will grow by _____.

5. The highest paid occupations in this chart are _____

_____.

A Write sentences using gerunds or infinitives. More than one answer is sometimes possible.

1. Joy / want / work / with children in a school

   _____

2. Min Hee / enjoy / help / patients in a hospital setting

   _____

3. Dan / need / make / a lot of money to support his family

   _____

4. Eduardo / not / want / work / on a computer all day

   _____

5. Jun / not / mind / take / risks

   _____

6. Luis / would like / learn / to cook at a culinary school

   _____

7. Maria Amelia / prefer / work / with co-workers

   _____

8. Feng / plan / follow / instructions carefully at her new job

   _____

9. Jean Paul / hope / become / an engineer

   _____

10. Alexandra / not / like / have / so many rules and regulations at work

    _____

B Read the conversation between Joy, a college student, and a career counselor. Circle the correct words to complete the sentences.

Mrs. Ito: Hello, Joy. Is this your first time at the TSU career center?

Joy: Yes, it's my first semester and I'd like **(to find out)** / **finding out** more about careers.

Mrs. Ito: OK. I have your interest survey. So you enjoy **to work** / **working** with children?

Joy: Yes. I have worked at a preschool. I **love** / **don't mind** to work with children.

Mrs. Ito: OK. So you might like **be** / **being** a teacher. What other jobs interest you?

Joy: I'm not sure, but I **want** / **avoid** to take risks, and I love challenges.

Mrs. Ito: Hmm. Have you considered **to study** / **studying** finance?

Joy: Well, I do need **to pay** / **paying** my loans after college, and I bet I'd make a lot of money. But I **don't like** / **don't mind** working on a computer all day.

Mrs. Ito: But there are many kinds of finance careers. Some involve **to work** / **working** with people. For example, you could become a financial consultant. They spend a lot of their time **talk** / **talking** to people, explaining how to borrow or manage money.

Joy: That sounds interesting. I guess I **would enjoy** / **would like** to learn more.

Mrs. Ito: OK, then you should plan ahead. Do you intend **to take** / **taking** math courses?

Joy: Yes, I plan **to take** / **taking** a calculus course this semester.

Mrs. Ito: Good. I also suggest taking a business course.

C MAKE IT PERSONAL. Write about yourself in your notebook. Use the words in the box.

> I would like . . .   I plan . . .   I enjoy . . .   I want . . .   I don't mind . . .

READ

Read the article. Highlight or underline the jobs mentioned and the specialized areas of those jobs.

Reading Skill:
Highlighting or underlining key information

As you read, highlight or underline key information that is especially useful for you. Generally, you should not highlight more than 10 percent of a text.

Be in Demand

When you look for a career, you need to think about your abilities and interests. You also have to think about what choices are realistic. For example, how much education or training does the job require? And you need to consider one more important thing: Will this job be in demand? Will you be able to find work doing this job or not? If the answer is no, try to find a related job that will be in demand.

When William Keenoy started his own construction business, he built new buildings. That was in 1994. He had fourteen employees and he wanted to keep them all. In 2002, he saw that new construction was declining. Then, by chance, a client asked him to work on a historical building. Keenoy's job was to repair the building to make it look like it had in the past. He noticed that there was a greater need for restoring old buildings than for building new ones. He changed the focus of his business. Now he specializes in restoration and he always has work.

You can do the same. Be flexible. You might want to be a teacher. You may have thought of teaching history,

William Keenoy

but will there be a need for history teachers? Not so much. On the other hand, there will be a high demand for math and science teachers over the next few years. Perhaps you are interested in finance. Jobs in banking, like financial analysts, are not going to increase in the next few years. However, people with both financial and technology skills will be in demand as more banks make online banking available.

Do your homework. Find a job that fits your interests and your skills, but make sure it is in demand. Look at the *Occupational Outlook Handbook* on the U.S. Department of Labor's website to find out the outlook for future jobs. Then see if you can develop skills in a specialized area of the job you want or find a related job instead. ■

CHECK YOUR UNDERSTANDING

A Write *T* (true) or *F* (false). Rewrite false statements to make them true.

_____ 1. William Keenoy owns his own business.

_____

_____ 2. William Keenoy specializes in new construction.

_____

_____ 3. In 1994, William Keenoy recognized that there would be less work in new construction.

_____

_____ 4. William Keenoy responded to the needs of the job market.

_____

_____ 5. In the future, there will be a high demand for history teachers.

_____

_____ 6. People who become math or science teachers will probably be able to find a job in the future.

_____

_____ 7. When the outlook is good for a career, this means the number of jobs in the area is growing.

_____

B Match the field with the specialties that will be in demand. Write the letters.

1. teaching: _b_, _____

2. construction: _____

3. banking: _____, _____

a. financial skills   c. restoration   e. technology skills
b. math   d. science

A Complete each sentence. Circle the correct answer.

1. I want to improve my computer skills _____ taking a class.

   a. about   b. by   c. for

2. Martin is good _____ speaking Chinese.

   a. at   b. of   c. in

3. Sofia is interested _____ learning English.

   a. to   b. in   c. of

4. Jae-Yong often thinks _____ becoming a chef.

   a. about   b. to   c. for

5. Kate thanked her career counselor _____ suggesting a helpful website.

   a. in   b. of   c. for

B Complete the paragraph. Write gerunds using the verbs in the box.

> apply   paint   reach   start   ~~work~~

I have been working as a painter for three years. I'm good at (1) _working_ with my hands, and I do fine work. Until now, I have worked for a subcontractor. But now I'm thinking about (2) _____ my own painting business. I plan on (3) _____ my cousins' and neighbors' houses this summer. Then I will have some references for my business. I'm also interested in (4) _____ for a bank loan to help start my own business. I want to start my new business next year. I'm excited about (5) _____ my goal!

C Complete the sentences with a preposition in the box and the correct form of the verb in parentheses.

> about   at   by   for   in   ~~of~~   on

1. I'm not afraid _____*of going*_____ (go) on a job interview.

2. Miriam is good _____ (listen) to other people.

3. Pawel thanked the career counselor _____ (help) him.

4. Prepare for the interview _____ (finish) your résumé.

5. I plan _____ (go) to the library to research jobs.

6. Leticia is interested _____ (take) computer courses.

7. Tonya is thinking _____ (study) dentistry.

D There are five mistakes. The first one is corrected. Find four more.

I work at a hospital and many of the patients speak Spanish. I am good at ~~learn~~ *learning* languages.

I speak Italian and English, so I think it will be easy to learn Spanish. I'm thinking about take

a class at a community center in my neighborhood. I'm also interested in find a person to

practice with. Maybe I can help that person by practice English. I plan on get as much

exposure to Spanish as I can. Eventually, I'll try reading Spanish magazines.

E MAKE IT PERSONAL. Write sentences in your notebook about yourself and your job or school goals. Use gerunds.

> *English is good for doing business.*

BEFORE YOU READ

Preview the article. Circle the main idea.

   a. Goals are easy to set.

   b. Goals can be adjusted if needed.

   c. Goals never work out as planned.

   d. Goals are easy to measure.

READ

Read the article.

> **Reading Skill:**
> Previewing
>
> Good readers preview a text before reading it more thoroughly. They look at photos, illustrations, graphs, or charts. They skim by looking over the text quickly to get the main idea. They pay special attention to the title and subtitles, the first sentence or two in each paragraph, and sometimes also the last sentence in each paragraph.

GOALS SET, BUT NOT MET

What do you do when you have been working toward a goal, and suddenly you find an obstacle in your way? Something unexpected is blocking your path. Now your goal looks unreachable. You begin to wonder if your goal ever *was* reachable. What do you do? How can you persist and not give up?

ASSESS YOUR GOAL

Don't despair and reject your goal outright. First assess what might be going wrong. Consider the following:

1. Make sure your goal is realistic. Ask yourself, "Is this really something I can achieve?"
2. Make sure your deadline is realistic. Ask yourself, "Did I give myself enough time to complete this goal?"
3. Look at what you are doing to reach your goal. Ask yourself, "Am I using all the resources available? Am I getting the skills I need to reach my goal? Is there a class I could take or an organization in my community that could help me?"

ADJUST YOUR GOAL

After you determine what is going wrong, don't give up. Make necessary adjustments. You might not need to set a new goal. You may just need to slightly alter your original goal. You can try the following strategies:

1. Adjust your goal if it wasn't realistic. Let's say that your dream was to buy a four-bedroom house in a particular area but you discover that the price for a house there is more than you can afford. You need to adjust your goal. For example, look at a smaller house or look in a less expensive neighborhood.
2. Adjust your deadline if it wasn't realistic. Perhaps you wanted to become a registered nurse. For this you need an associate's degree in nursing. You gave yourself two years. Then you realized you can't study full-time. You may need to change your deadline to three or four years instead.
3. Rethink the steps you are taking to reach your goal. Maybe you are not taking the correct steps. Think about what other steps might be more effective, and then take those steps.

Remember: Don't simply give up. Make adjustments and continue working to reach your goal.

CHECK YOUR UNDERSTANDING

A Match the subtitles from the article with the description. Write the letters.

1. _____ Assess your goal

2. _____ Adjust your goal

a. Take steps to change your goal and make it more realistic

b. Ask yourself questions if you're not reaching your goal

B Complete the statements. Circle the correct answer.

1. If something gets in the way of reaching a goal, you should _____.

   a. decide it's not worth reaching

   b. question whether it was reachable

2. If you cannot meet a goal, you should _____.

   a. figure out why

   b. change your goal completely

3. If the deadline for your goal is not realistic, you should _____.

   a. give up

   b. change the deadline

4. Before you adjust your goal, you should _____.

   a. take a class

   b. ask yourself questions about it

C Check (✓) all the ways you can adjust a goal. Look at the article to check your answers.

_____ change the deadline

_____ find a way to get a skill you need to reach the goal

_____ don't measure the goal

_____ reject it

_____ make someone help you

_____ change the way you reach the goal

DICTIONARY SKILL: Understanding a dictionary entry

Ⓐ Knowing how to use a dictionary will help you expand your vocabulary. Read the dictionary entry for the word *category*. Look at the labels to identify the parts of the entry.

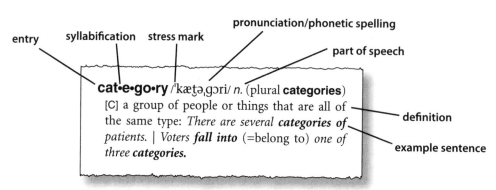

Ⓑ Study the labels again. Answer the questions about the dictionary entry.

1. You want to know how the word *category* is used in a sentence. Which part of the entry should you look at?

_____

2. You want to know whether the word is a noun, adjective, verb, or some other part of speech. Which part of the dictionary entry should you look at?

_____

3. You want to know how to pronounce the word *category*. Which three parts of the entry should you look at?

_____

4. To find out how many syllables *category* has, which part of the entry should you look at?

_____

5. You don't know which syllable gets the main stress in *category*. Which part of the entry tells you this?

_____

WORD STUDY: Learning prefixes and suffixes

Knowing the meanings of common **prefixes** and **suffixes** will help you figure out the meanings of many words.

A **prefix** is a group of letters added to the beginning of a word that changes the meaning of the word. For example, a common prefix in English is *dis-*. *Dis-* can mean "not," "outside of," or "the opposite of."

A Look at the chart. Add the prefix *dis-* to each base word to create a new word. Write the new word and its meaning in the chart.

Prefix	Base word	New word	Definition
1. dis-	allow	disallow	not allow
2. dis-	approve	disapprove	not approve
3. dis-	continue		
4. dis-	agree		

A **suffix** is a letter or group of letters added to the end of a word. It can change the part of speech and meaning of a word. For example, the suffix *-able* means "able to be, give, or do."

B Look at the chart. Add the suffix *-able* to each base word to create a new word. Write the new word and its meaning in the chart.

Base word	Suffix	New word	Meaning
1. measure	-able	measurable	able to be measured
2. enjoy	-able	enjoyable	giving pleasure
3. exchange	-able		
4. accept	-able		

C Create a new word by adding the prefix *dis-* or the suffix *-able* to each word. Then write the definition. Use a dictionary if necessary.

1. trust _____

2. obey _____

3. afford _____

A Read the descriptive essay. Then look at the sentences below. Which two sentences fit the paragraphs? Write the number (*1* or *2*) next to the correct topic sentence.

My dream is to work in the ER of a hospital. I want to work in the ER because it is a place where I can make a difference and help my community. Right now, I work at South Miami Hospital as a medical assistant. To work in the ER, you usually need to be a registered nurse, so I am getting my RN license. The ER is not an easy unit to work in, but I think I have two important qualifications.

First of all, (1) _____. The ER is a stressful environment, but I can deal with stress well and make fast decisions. I also have good judgment in a crisis.

Second, (2) _____. In the ER, nurses need to assist physicians during surgeries, treatments, and exams. They also need to administer medications. I can follow instructions well, and I speak English and Spanish, so I can communicate with doctors and patients who might not speak each other's languages.

My dream is to be a strong advocate and health educator for patients, families, and communities. In the ER, I can fulfill my dream and help a lot of people.

_____ I have a lot of experience working in the ER.
_____ I have good communication skills.
_____ I want to be a health educator.
_____ I am very calm and a good problem solver.

B Look at the essay again. Underline the descriptive sentences that support the topic sentences.

REVIEW & EXPAND: Vocabulary

A Match the words with their definitions. Write the letters.

_____ 1. category

_____ 2. occupation

_____ 3. statistics

_____ 4. imagination

_____ 5. numerous

a. many

b. numbers that represent facts or measurements

c. job or profession

d. a group of people or things that are all of the same type

e. ability to form pictures or ideas in your mind

Learning Strategy:
Vocabulary cards

Making vocabulary cards is a good way to learn and remember new words.

B Study the card made by a Russian student for the word *imagination.* Then make vocabulary cards for the words in Exercise A. Use this card as a model and add a picture to each card.

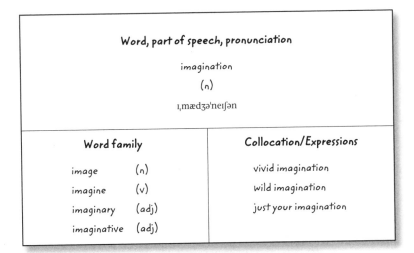

Word, part of speech, pronunciation

imagination

(n)

ɪ,mædʒəˈneɪʃən

Word family		Collocation/Expressions
image	(n)	vivid imagination
imagine	(v)	wild imagination
imaginary	(adj)	just your imagination
imaginative	(adj)	

First language translation for *imagination*: фантазия (in Russian)	
English definition ability to form pictures or ideas in your mind	**Example sentence** Use your imagination to think of your dream job.

BEFORE YOU READ

Have you ever thought about volunteering? Some people volunteer at an organization to gain job skills.

READ

Read the article.

> ### Reading Skill:
> Use prior knowledge
>
> Before you read a text, ask yourself, "What do I already know about this topic?" Connecting the text to your prior knowledge will help you understand and remember what you read. Also, identifying what you already know may help you realize what you *don't* know. This prepares you to look for new information.

Choosing a VOLUNTEER OPPORTUNITY

Most people need a well paying job now. Why then volunteer, and how can it help you? First, if you are just entering the workforce or if you are changing jobs, volunteering can give you experience to put on your résumé. Second, volunteering is helpful to people who have been out of the workforce for a while or who are in between jobs. When people look for a job, they need recent experience to add to their résumé. Volunteering makes people more desirable to employers because it shows they are active in the workforce.

What are the obastacles?

The biggest obstacle to volunteering is finding time. If you have one or more jobs or if you have a family, it may be nearly impossible to volunteer. However, volunteering does not have to mean too many hours. You can volunteer five hours a week, or less. You can also volunteer for a single event like a fundraiser and still put it on your résumé.

What kind of volunteer work should you do?

Determine the job you would like to have in the future. Then determine what volunteer position will give you the experience, skills, or information you want to find out about the job. Let's say you would like to become a medical technician.

To do that, you must have a bachelor's degree. But it would also help to have direct experience. You can volunteer in a hospital at a blood bank. Volunteering will help you learn what goes on day to day. This not only gives you experience but also will help you know if you are really interested in the field.

Where can you volunteer?

Many institutions have existing volunteer organizations, for example: schools, hospitals, libraries, senior care facilities, city run organizations, and not-for-profit organizations, like food pantries. These organizations are ready for volunteers and provide training. Community websites are a good place to start your research.

Finally, aside from gaining marketable skills and experience, volunteering can fulfill a dream. For example, some people might volunteer to help the sick or to help their community. Marianne Diaz started an organization to help with gang recovery. She grew up in a neighborhood with gangs. Marianne wanted to give hope to young people who were trying to leave gangs. By volunteering, Marianne gained organizational, management, and fundraising skills, and she helped her community.

CHECK YOUR UNDERSTANDING

A **Read the article again. Then circle the best answer to each question.**

1. Why does volunteering help people who have been out of work?

    a. It makes them feel good about themselves.

    b. They can put it on a résumé.

2. How does volunteering help people who are between jobs?

    a. It makes them look active in the workforce.

    b. They are helping their community.

3. What is the most difficult thing about volunteering?

    a. researching volunteer jobs

    b. finding the time to volunteer

4. What kind of volunteer work should you choose?

    a. a field in which you have no experience

    b. a field in which you would like to work in the future

5. What are three things you get from volunteer work?

    a. skills, experience, and answers to questions you might have about a job

    b. skills, experience, and a job at a company

6. What are positive things Marianne Diaz got from volunteering?

    a. skills and a paying job in her community

    b. skills and a feeling of giving back to the community

B **Answer the questions.**

1. What are some places that usually have volunteering programs?

    _____

2. Why did Marianne Diaz volunteer?

    _____

C **MAKE IT PERSONAL. Choose a workplace mentioned in the article or use your own idea. In the notebook, write three skills you might learn by volunteering there.**

LIFE SKILLS

A Read the résumé. Find and correct six spelling mistakes.

Mark Fiore

704 Oak Street, Bakersfield, 93301   Home: 555-765-6507   E-mail:

Desired Ocupation: Chef

Education: Bachelor of Arts, Culinary Arts, 2005, Sonoma Culinary Institute, CA

Skills:

➤ Experienced in fast-paced high-volume restaurants

➤ Skilled at menu planning

➤ Efficient at cost control

Experence:

Cook, Dec. 2005–Jan. 2006 King Restaurant, Los Angeles, CA

➤ Prepared meals for brekfasts, lunches, and dinners

➤ Made Chinese dishes and seafood

➤ Cooked on the line and handled pasta station

➤ Helped with ordering and recieving of supplies

Chef, 2006–2010 Good Appetite, Los Angeles, CA

➤ Developed new dinner and lunch menus for the resteraunt

➤ Maintained food cost analysis, inventory, budgeting, and purchasing

---

B Read the résumé again and answer these questions:

Is the information in the correct order? What information is missing from the résumé?

_____

_____

STUDY SKILL: Read a bar graph

Look at the graph. Complete the sentences.

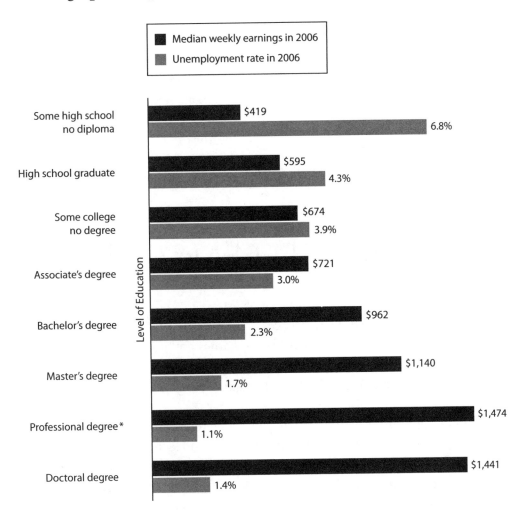

Legend:
- Median weekly earnings in 2006
- Unemployment rate in 2006

Level of Education:

- Some high school no diploma: $419, 6.8%
- High school graduate: $595, 4.3%
- Some college no degree: $674, 3.9%
- Associate's degree: $721, 3.0%
- Bachelor's degree: $962, 2.3%
- Master's degree: $1,140, 1.7%
- Professional degree*: $1,474, 1.1%
- Doctoral degree: $1,441, 1.4%

* A professional degree is a degree that allows you to work in a certain profession, such as law or medicine. An example of a professional degree is an MD, or a doctor of medicine.

Source: U.S. Bureau of Labor Statistics

1. In 2006, on average, a high school graduate earned $_____ a week.

2. A person with a bachelor's degree earned $_____ a week.

3. A person with a(n) _____ degree earned the most in 2006.

4. The unemployment rate for people with an associate's degree was _____ percent.

5. The unemployment rate was the lowest for someone with a(n) _____ degree.

6. The unemployment rate for people with an associate's degree was _____ percent lower than for people with no high school diploma.

READ

Read the article. Compare Hector and Eva. Who had better references?

> **Reading Skill:**
> Comparing and contrasting
>
> Making comparisons and contrasts helps you understand a text better. When you compare, you notice how things are similar. When you contrast, you look at how they are different.

BE REFERENCE READY

In your résumé, you need to include references—people that an employer can contact to find out about you. It's standard to include the names and contact information of three people who can comment on your work performance and **character**. Compare Hector's and Eva's references. What did they do right or wrong?

Hector applied for a **manufacturing** job. He gave three references. The first reference was an employer who liked Hector but was not happy with Hector's job performance. Hector had been **chronically** late to work and was often sick. This employer **verified** that Hector worked for him but did not give him a recommendation. Hector's second reference was an employer who had closed his business. Hector did not know this, so when the manufacturer called the reference, he got a wrong phone number. The third reference Hector gave was a co-worker. This co-worker said positive things about Hector's character, but did not know much about Hector's work. This coworker was also a cousin. As a result, the manufacturer did not take this reference seriously.

Eva also applied for a job and gave three references. They all checked out well. Her first reference was an employer who knew the quality of her work and recommended her. The second reference was a building manager Eva had worked for part-time. He said that Eva was reliable. The third reference was a teacher at Miami Dade Adult High School who said that Eva was organized and completed assignments on time. The teacher gave Eva a good reference but was a bit surprised when she received the call. Eva had not called her beforehand to ask if she would give a reference.

Remember, when you give references, make sure to give accurate contact information and give only the names of people who think highly of your work.

CHECK YOUR UNDERSTANDING

A **Read the statements. Write *T* (true) or *F* (false).**

_____ 1. Hector gave correct contact information.

_____ 2. Eva gave correct contact information.

_____ 3. Hector's past employer said that Hector had worked for him.

_____ 4. Hector's past employer gave him a good reference.

_____ 5. Eva did not have three work references.

_____ 6. Eva's references were all good.

B **Match the boldfaced words from the article with the definitions. Write the letters.**

_____ 1. character   a. very often and over a long period of time

_____ 2. chronically   b. confirmed that something is true

_____ 3. manufacturing   c. the qualities that a person has, like honesty

_____ 4. verified   d. a job area where people make goods in factories

C **Rate the references. Write *1* for excellent reference(s), or *2* for good reference(s). Write *0* (zero) if the reference is not good.**

References
_____ **Your current employer.**   You have worked there for three months. Your employer does not know that you plan to leave.
_____ **A former co-worker who is now a manager at your old company.**   The co-worker knows your work well and supported you at your previous job.
_____ **An employer you worked for two years ago.**   You came to work on time. Your work was high quality and you got good reviews.
_____ **An employer you worked for part-time five years ago.**   You were reliable and came to work on time.
_____ **A close friend of the family.**   He or she has known you for your whole life.

A Complete the paragraph. Use the present perfect form of the verb.

The restaurant where Mark was working just closed, so he needs a new job. He _____ (**1. not / find**) a job yet, but he should be able to soon. Mark has many job qualifications to be a chef. He _____ (**2. work**) in restaurants for five years. He _____ (**3. prepare**) meals for large numbers of people and _____ (**4. write**) menus. Mark _____ (**5. cook**) many different types of food, such as Chinese, Italian, and Californian cuisine. He _____ (**6. complete**) an associate's degree in culinary arts. He _____ (**7. pass**) tests in sanitation and he _____ (**8. receive**) a food safety certification.

B Look at the list. Write sentences about what Mark has and hasn't done to find a job.

✓	write a résumé	✓	look for volunteer work
___	send copies of my résumé to employers	___	start volunteer work
✓	research jobs online		

1. <u>Mark has written a résumé.</u>

2. _____

3. _____

4. _____

5. _____

C Look at Bi-Yun's calendar. Today is Friday. Complete the sentences. Use the present perfect and *for*.

Monday	Tuesday	Wednesday	Thursday
moved to Dallas to find work	started volunteering daily at an organization called Helping Hands	got on a waiting list for a computer training course	met Ms. Neves, a career counselor, for the first time

1. Bi-Yun _____*has lived*_____ (live) in Dallas _____*for four days*_____.

2. She _____ (be) on a waiting list for a computer course

   _____.

3. She _____ (know) Ms. Neves _____.

4. She _____ (volunteer) at Helping Hands _____.

D Write sentences with the verb provided. Use the present perfect and *since*.

1. Hilda started working in hospitals when she was a teenager. (work)

   Hilda has worked in hospitals since she was a teenager.

2. Dadi bought his computer in 2006. (have)

   _____

3. Carla moved here in 1997. (live)

   _____

4. Mr. and Mrs. Pham met Veronica in September. (know)

   _____

5. Manuel trained as an HVAC technician in the Fall. (be)

   _____

DICTIONARY SKILL: Using word order and guide words

In a dictionary, words, expressions, and abbreviations are arranged in alphabetical order. For example:

a•bate /əˈbeɪt/ v. [I] (formal) to become less strong → UNABATED: *Public anger does not appear to be abating.*
ab•bey /ˈæbi/ n. [C] a large church, with buildings next to it where MONKS and NUNS live [ORIGIN: 1200–1300 Old French *abaïe*, from late Latin *abbas*, from Aramaic *abba* "father"]
ab•bre•vi•ate /əˈbriviˌeɪt/ v. [T] (formal) to make a word, story, etc. shorter: *"Street" is often abbreviated as "St."* [Origin: 1400–1500 late Latin, past participle of *abbreviare*, from Latin *brevis* "short"]

ab•bre•vi•a•tion /əˌbriviˈeɪʃən/ n. [C] the short form a of a word used in writing. For example, *Mr.* is the abbreviation of *Mister.*
ABC n. 1 **ABC's** [plural] the letters of the English alphabet as taught to children 2 **American Broadcasting Company** one of the national companies that broadcasts television and radio programs in the U.S.
ab•di•cate /ˈæbdɪˌkeɪt/ v. 1 [I,T] to officially give up the position of being king or queen 2 **abdicate (your) responsibility** (formal) to refuse to continue being responsible for something

Ⓐ **Look at these words and expressions. Decide how they would be ordered in a dictionary. Number them from *1–9*. Check your answers in a dictionary.**

_____ John Doe   _____ judo   _____ jigsaw puzzle

_____ journalist   _____ jeans   _____ jet set

_____ justice   _____ justice of the peace   _____ jazz

Guide words appear at the top corner of each page. They tell you the first and last words on these pages to help you find the entry you want. Look at the guide words for pages 450–451 of the *Longman Dictionary of American English* (LDAE).

however	
however² conjunction in whatever way: *However you do it, I'm sure it will be good.*	

	humility
	hu•mil•i•ty // n. [U] approving the quality of not being too proud about yourself

Ⓑ **Look at the guide words above for pages 450–451. Then circle the words below that you think can be found on these pages.**

how   howl   hubcap   human   humor

WORD STUDY: Understanding multiple-meaning words

Many words in English have more than one meaning. They also can have more than one part of speech. Look at the different meanings and parts of speech for the word *season*.

Sentence	Part of Speech	Word and Meaning
The winter **season** is cold here.	**noun**	***season*** = one of the four main periods in the year
We plan to **season** the turkey with rosemary.	**verb**	***season*** = add salt, pepper, and other spices to make something taste good

When you read, remember that a word might have several meanings. To know which meaning is being used, look at the sentence. Try to guess the part of speech. Then look at all the definitions for the word in the dictionary. Choose the definition that makes the most sense for the context.

Look at the sentences in the chart below. Write the meanings and parts of speech of each boldfaced word. Use a dictionary to check your answers.

Multiple-Meaning Word	Part of Speech	Meaning
1. We had a minor car **crash** on Monday. **2.** What should I do when the office computers **crash**?	1. noun 2. verb	1. accident 2. suddenly stop working
3. I made a good **impression** at the job interview. **4.** The table leg left an **impression** in the rug.		
5. Ilhan will **supply** a cover letter with his résumé. **6.** The paper **supply** in the office is running out.		
7. Josie's friendliness has a positive **impact** on her customers. **8.** Changing technology **impacts** all areas of the job market.		

A Rewrite the sentences. Use the present perfect continuous.

1. Jim has worked at a bank since 1992.

   Jim has been working at a bank since 1992.

2. Hassan and Penelope have studied English for three years.

   _____

3. Te-Chao hasn't studied English for long.

   _____

4. Victoria and Kyle have used the Internet all day.

   _____

5. I've written my résumé.

   _____

B Write one new sentence from the information provided. Use the present perfect or the present perfect continuous. Add *since* when necessary.

1. I started looking for work in November. I'm still looking for work.

   I've been looking for work since November.

2. Ben learned new computer skills for his job. Now he might get a promotion.

   Ben has learned new computer skills.

3. Kamila started studying Spanish in 2007. She is still studying it.

   _____

4. Jenni took an Excel 1 computer class in the fall. Now she is taking Excel 2.

   _____

5. Ms. Rios and Mr. Lee interviewed four people for the job. They just finished the interviews.

   _____

6. Roberto practiced for his job interview. Now he feels confident and ready.

   _____

C Read about Dress for Success®. Circle the correct verb forms. More than one answer is sometimes possible.

Dress for Success® is a company that gives professional clothing to women who do not have enough money to buy them. Where does Dress for Success® get its clothing? Both volunteers and clothing companies **have given / have been giving** suits to the organization in the past. The company **has helped / has been helping** over 450,000 women so far. Dress for Success® **has also started / has also been starting** a career center. Since it started, women **have learned / have been learning** computer skills to help them search for jobs.

Nancy Lubin started the company in 1996 in the United States. Since then, it **has expanded / has been expanding** to four other countries. Joi Gordon **has worked / has been working** as the executive director of Dress for Success® Worldwide since 2002. She now has a staff of over 50,000 people. In addition, many volunteers **have worked / have been working** at Dress for Success® over the years.

D MAKE IT PERSONAL. Answer the questions. Use the present perfect or the present perfect continuous.

1. How long have you been studying English? Where have you been studying?

_____

2. Have you interviewed for a job in the last six months?

_____

3. Have you had a job in the past year? Where have you been working?

_____

4. Have you volunteered before? Where have you volunteered?

_____

5. Have you ever taken a computer course? How long have you been using the Internet?

_____

Read the job ad and the e-mail cover letter. Underline the words or ideas in the letter that match the language in the job ad.

New Modern Latin Downtown Restaurant (Downtown Los Angeles)

Reply to: job-923042366@craiglist.org
Date: 2008-11-17, 12:56PM PST

Line cook, full-time position

Responsibilities:
-Cook on the line
-Maintain safety and sanitation standards of kitchen and equipment
-Assist in menu planning and creation of menu items

Job requirements: Minimum of 3 years experience, knowledge of sanitation requirements and food handling safety standards. Knowledge of purchasing, inventory controls, supplies, and equipment. Excellent communication skills a must. Positive attitude.

E-mail cover letter and attach résumé

To Whom It May Concern:

I am writing in response to your ad for a line cook. My education and qualifications make me a great match for this position.

As you can see from my attached résumé, I have five years of relevant experience. I understand cost analysis and have produced cost-effective, quality dishes. I also know budgeting and purchasing procedures.

In addition to these qualifications, I have the ability to plan menus and invent new dishes. I am a graduate of Sonoma Culinary Institute, and I have a talent for creating new recipes. Finally, I am safety certified. I look forward to hearing from you. Thank you for your consideration.

Oscar Sanchez

A Match the words with their definitions. Write the letters.

_____ 1. employment agency

_____ 2. document

_____ 3. customer

_____ 4. ambitious

_____ 5. retail

_____ 6. human resources (HR) department

a. piece of paper that has official information written on it

b. someone who buys things from a store or company

c. referring to goods or services that are sold for personal use

d. section of a company that deals with employing, training, and helping employees

e. having a strong desire to be successful or powerful

f. business that makes money by finding jobs for people

B Use words from Exercise A to complete the sentences.

1. The counselor at the _____ helped Jenny with her job search.

2. Ricardo has applied for a higher-level job; he is very _____ and wants to rise in the company.

3. To solve a problem with a co-worker, Ricardo went to the _____.

4. Sabra has a lot of _____ experience. She was a cashier at a pharmacy and a gift shop.

C Look at the words in Exercise A. Which words fit the category *sales*? Which fit the category *employment*? Find two examples of each. Write in your notebook.

Learning Strategy:
Categorizing words

Categorizing words is a good way to learn words and remember their meanings. It helps you understand situations in which the words often appear.

Expansion: Dictionary Skills and Word Study

DICTIONARY SKILL: Learning dictionary abbreviations

Knowing the meaning of abbreviations and labels in a dictionary will help you use it effectively. Read the sample abbreviations and labels from *The Longman Dictionary of American English* (LDAE).

Short forms used in the dictionary

Parts of Speech

Some parts of speech have short forms:

adj.	adjective	*prep.*	preposition
adv.	adverb	*pron.*	pronoun
n.	noun	*v.*	verb
phr. v.	phrasal verb		

Other short forms

etc.	et cetera (= and so on)
U.S.	United States
s/he	she or he
sb	somebody/someone
sth	something
sb/sth	somebody or something

Study the dictionary abbreviations and labels. Answer the questions.

> **dis·tract·ed** /dɪ'stræktɪd/ *adj.* anxious and not able to think clearly.

> **driv·er** /'draɪvɚ/ *n.* [C] **1** someone who drives. *a truck/cab/bus* **driver** | *Joyce is a good/bad* **driver.** **2** *IT* a piece of software that makes a computer work with another piece of equipment such as a PRINTER or a MOUSE.

> **i·den·ti·fy** /aɪ'dɛntə'faɪ, ɪ-/ *v.* **identified**, **identifies** [T] to recognize and name someone or something: *Can you* **identify** *the man who robbed you?*
> **identify with** sb/sth *phr. v.* **1 identify with** sb to be able to share or understand the feelings of someone else: *It was easy to* **identify with** *the novel's main character.* **2 be identified with** sb/sth to be closely connected with an idea or organization: *He will always* **be identified with** *the Harry Potter movies.*

1. Which entry word is a noun? _____

2. Which entry word is an adjective? _____

3. Which entry word is a verb? _____

4. What part of speech is *identify with*? _____

5. What does the abbreviation *sb* mean after *identify with*? _____

WORD STUDY: Understanding compound nouns

English contains many compound nouns. A compound noun is made up of more than one word. Some of these nouns are written as one word, as in *windshield, dashboard,* or *airbag.* Some are written as two or more words, as in *seat belt,* or *tow truck operator.* Others are written with hyphens, as in *father-in-law.*

If you are not sure how to spell a compound noun, check a dictionary. If the compound noun is not in a large dictionary, it is most likely spelled as two or more separate words.

Complete the compound nouns with words in the box. Check the correct spelling in a dictionary. More than one answer may be possible.

brake	jam	light	mirror	patrol
pedal	phone	shift	~~wheel~~	wiper

1. steering *wheel*

2. head

3. windshield

4. rearview

5. cell

6. emergency

7. gas

8. gear

9. highway

10. traffic

BEFORE YOU READ

Look at the parts of the car, the equipment, and their names.

1. hubcap
2. screwdriver
3. tire
4. lug wrench
5. carjack
6. lug nuts
7. wheel chock

READ

Read the article. After you read each paragraph, repeat the information in your own words.

> **Reading Skill:**
> Paraphrasing
>
> When you read, it's helpful to pause occasionally and try to repeat information in your own words. This will help you to recognize places where you have trouble understanding the text. It will also give you an opportunity to practice producing language about the topic, and it will help you to remember information from the text.

how to

Getting a flat tire while driving is a common problem, so if you drive often, it's likely to happen to you. You can call roadside assistance, but it's good to know how to change a flat tire yourself. Here are some simple steps. Make sure you practice so that you know you can do it correctly before it happens.

1. Before you drive, make sure you always have the necessary equipment in your vehicle. Know where your spare tire is, and make sure it isn't flat. Be sure to have a lug wrench, a screwdriver, a carjack (a device for raising the car), and reflecting triangles.

2. When you get a flat, signal with your turn signal and pull off the road. Turn on your emergency flashers. Put reflecting triangles behind your vehicle to alert other drivers.

3. If you have young children with you, make sure they are out of the vehicle before you change the tire. Also, make sure they are out of the way of traffic.

4. Put a large rock in front of or behind one of the tires if you are on a hill. This will stop your vehicle from moving while you're changing the tire. You might want to keep a wheel chock in your vehicle in case you are ever in an area where you can't find a rock.

5. Remove the hubcap with the screwdriver. Then loosen the lug nuts with the lug wrench. (This makes it easier to remove them later.)

6. Use the carjack to raise your vehicle. Make sure the carjack is placed correctly and safely.

7. Remove the lug nuts with the wrench, and remove the tire.

8. Put your spare tire on the car. Put the lug nuts back on loosely.

9. Lower the carjack. Once your vehicle is on the ground, tighten the lug nuts with the wrench.

10. Put the hubcap back on.

Before you leave, check quickly to make sure everything is correct and tight. And don't forget to take your old tire with you. You may be able to have it repaired.

CHECK YOUR UNDERSTANDING

Answer the questions.

1. What can you do if you get a flat tire and don't know how to change it?

    _____

2. Why should you practice changing a flat tire?

    _____

3. What do you need to keep in your vehicle?

    _____

4. If there are children in the car, where should they be while you change the tire?

    _____

5. When should you use the wrench to tighten the lug nuts?

    _____

6. What should you do after changing the tire, before you get back in your vehicle?

    _____

A Complete the paragraph. Use the correct form of the verbs in the box.

break down	figure out	flag down
jack up	pull over	~~run into~~

You should always be prepared in case you (1) _____run into_____ trouble on the road. You

should keep an emergency kit in your vehicle. Include things that will help if your vehicle

(2) _____. For example, include tools such as a wrench and a screwdriver. Make sure

you have a carjack in case you need to (3) _____ your vehicle to change a flat. You

might also want to include reflecting triangles, a white cloth, and a flashlight. Include a map of

your area. This will help you (4) _____ where to go if you get lost. If you have car

trouble, make sure to (5) _____ to the shoulder. Never (6) _____ a

stranger for help. Always take a cell phone with you if you have one.

B Complete the sentences. Make phrasal verbs with the words in the box.

down   in   ~~into~~   on   out   over   up

1. Be careful not to get _____into_____ a car if the driver is drunk.

2. Make sure to slow _____ if it starts to rain.

3. I got _____ of my car to change the tire.

4. My engine light came _____ while I was driving.

5. Remember to always check _____ your side mirror when you change lanes.

6. If your car starts to overheat, you should pull _____ to the shoulder.

7. It's starting to rain. Please roll _____ the window.

C Rewrite the sentences. Replace the boldfaced objects with the object pronouns *it, them, her,* or *him.*

1. Make sure you fill **the tank** up.

   Make sure you fill it up.

2. There's no room for passengers, so you need to clean **the car** out.

   _____

3. It's starting to rain, so turn the **windshield wipers** on.

   _____

4. Ivan picked **Galina** up and they went for a drive.

   _____

5. When we stopped at a rest stop, I let **my dog Sam** out of the car.

   _____

6. Have you figured **the directions** out yet, or are we still lost?

   _____

D Some of the sentences have phrasal verbs and particles that can be separated. Rewrite only those sentences.

1. I have to pick up my brother at 3:00.

   I have to pick my brother up at 3:00.

2. Julie turns on her lights when she drives at night.

   _____

3. Did Guy think over the problem carefully?

   _____

4. Eric needs to go over traffic rules before he takes his driving test.

   _____

5. I got out of my car to change the tire.

   _____

E MAKE IT PERSONAL. In your notebook, write about a time when you or someone you know had trouble in a car or a bus.

LIFE SKILLS

The State of California has a program to help income-eligible drivers get low-cost automobile insurance for under $400 a year (liability only). Look at the chart. Then write what each person's premium will be.

Income Eligibility

HOUSEHOLD SIZE	MAXIMUM INCOME
1 PERSON	$25,525
2 PEOPLE	$34,225
3 PEOPLE	$42,925
4 PEOPLE	$51,625
5 PEOPLE	$60,325
6 PEOPLE	$69,025
7 PEOPLE	$77,725
8 PEOPLE	$86,425

County Premiums

County	Premium	County	Premium
Alameda	$318.00	San Bernardino	$280.00
Contra Costa	$313.00	San Diego	$265.00
Fresno	$295.00	San Francisco	$336.00
Imperial	$208.00	San Joaquin	$292.00
Kern	$236.00	San Mateo	$303.00
Los Angeles	$350.00	Santa Barbara	$220.00
Merced	$267.00	Santa Clara	$286.00
Monterey	$210.00	Sonoma	$270.00
Orange	$308.00	Stanislaus	$354.00
Riverside	$243.00	Tulare	$222.00
Sacramento	$378.00	Ventura	$280.00

Source: © 2008 California Department of Insurance

	Who	Number of people in household	County	Income	Premium per person
1.	Graciela and Diego Rivera	2	Santa Clara	$32,500	$286.00
2.	Lan, Tu, and Uyen Fan	3	Monterey	$37,925	
3.	the Chens	6	San Mateo	$58,700	
4.	Lucilea Brito	1	Sacramento	$25,250	
5.	the Sokolovs	4	Los Angeles	$49,000	
6.	the Kennedys	8	Ventura	$86,425	

STUDY SKILL: Read an insurance card

A Look at the insurance identification card. Circle the name of the insurance company.

NEW YORK STATE INSURANCE IDENTIFICATION CARD		
USA CASUALTY INSURANCE COMPANY 980 Frederick Road ▪ San Antonio, TX 78788	Policy Number RENEWAL 00995 39 58B	THIS ID CARD MUST BE CARRIED IN THE INSURED VEHICLE FOR PRODUCTION UPON DEMAND.
An authorized NEW YORK insurer has issued an Owner's Policy of Liability Insurance complying with Article 6 (Motor Vehicle Financial Security Act) of the New York Vehicle and Traffic Law to:	Effective Date Expiration Date 12/05/2010 12/05/2011 12:01 A.M. 12:01 A.M. Applicable with respect to the following Motor Vehicle:	WARNING: Any person who issues or produces an ID card knowing that an Owner's Policy of Insurance is not in effect may be committing a misdemeanor. In addition, a person who presents an ID card if insurance is not in effect may be committing a misdemeanor.
TATIANA ROSTOV 3878 Lyme Avenue Brighton Beach, NY 11224	2000 DODGE Year Make 1C4VP45L9WC506923 Vehicle Identification Number	The name of the registrant and the name of the insured must coincide.
	FOR POLICY SERVICE, CALL 1-555-530-8111 FOR AUTO/PROPERTY CLAIMS, CALL 1-555-530-8222	

B Answer the questions about the insurance card.

1. What is the name of the policy owner?

   _____

2. Where does this card need to be carried?

   _____

3. What make of car is the policy for?

   _____

4. When does the insurance policy start and end?

   _____

5. What number does the policy owner need to call to file a claim?

   _____

BEFORE YOU READ

Look at the illustration. When drivers look in their side-view mirrors, they have a blind spot. That is an area they can't see in the mirrors. When you change lanes or pull out, you need to turn your head briefly to check your blind spot.

READ

Read the article.

DANGEROUS DISTRACTIONS

Driving distractions lead to many accidents. There are many kinds of driving distractions, such as putting on makeup or text messaging. The following drivers could have taken precautions and avoided accidents:

Maria was driving downtown and stopped at an intersection as the light turned red. While she was stopped, her cell phone rang. She picked it up and answered the call. As she did, she stopped watching the signal. The signal changed to green, and the car behind her accelerated and hit Maria's car.

Ivan was driving his car at night. The car in front was driving quickly, but Ivan wanted to pass it. He pulled into his left lane to pass. As he was driving in the left lane, he lit a cigarette. Because he was focused on his cigarette, he forgot to check his rear blind spot to see if he had passed the other car. He pulled into the right-hand lane where the other car still was and slammed into it.

Dipak was driving a customer back from the airport. The customer did not know the directions, and Dipak had to look at a map. Instead of pulling the taxi over, he continued to drive and glanced down at the map every few seconds. Suddenly he saw a motorcycle slow down in front of him. Dipak slammed on the brakes, turned the wheel, and drove off the city street onto a curb, smashing into a fire hydrant.

Good driving requires a driver's complete attention. Avoid being a distracted driver. Follow these tips:

- Always avoid multi-tasking. Do not eat, drink, or reach for anything in your car while you drive. Pull off the road when you need to eat or look at a map.

- Do not talk on a cell phone. Even hands-free devices do not make cell phones safe while driving. It is best to turn off the cell phone before you drive so that you will not answer any calls. Also, do not send text messages.

CHECK YOUR UNDERSTANDING

A Look at the article. Which event happened first? Number the events in order.

_____ The car behind Maria hit her.

_____ The signal turned green.

_____ Maria answered a call on her cell phone.

__1__ The signal turned red.

_____ The car behind Maria accelerated.

Reading Skill:
Understanding and sequencing

Knowing the sequence, or order, of events in a text will help you understand and remember what you read. Look for clues that show sequence, such as the words *first, next, before, later,* and *finally.* Also look for dates, days of the week, and times of the year.

B Number the events in order.

_____ Ivan smashed into the other car.

_____ Ivan pulled into the right-hand lane.

_____ Ivan was driving behind a car.

_____ Ivan lit a cigarette.

_____ Ivan pulled into the left-hand lane to pass the car in front.

C Number the events in order.

_____ Dipak drove off the city street.

_____ Dipak drove over a curb and hit a fire hydrant.

_____ Dipak noticed a motorcycle in front of his car.

_____ Dipak left the airport to take a customer home.

_____ Dipak slammed on the brakes and turned the wheel.

_____ Dipak looked down at a map.

D MAKE IT PERSONAL. Have you ever been distracted while you were driving? What were you doing? Write in your notebook.

LIFE SKILLS

You are driving to a friend's house in Queens, New York. Look at the map and complete the directions below. Circle the correct words.

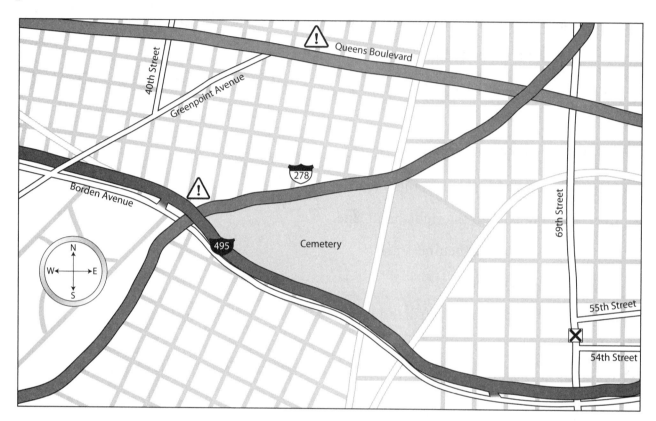

1. You are going from 40th Street to 69th Street, between 54th and 55th Avenues. Queens Boulevard has a lot of traffic, so you decide you want to take **I-495 / I-278**.

2. To get there, you go **south / north** on 40th Street. Then you make a **left / right** onto Greenpoint Avenue.

3. Next, you make a **left / right** onto Borden Avenue. Borden Avenue is the service road for **I-495/I-278.**

4. Before you get on the ramp to enter I-495, you see that traffic is moving **slowly / quickly** on I-495, so you stay on Borden Avenue.

5. You go **west / east** on Borden Avenue. You pass **the cemetery / Queens Boulevard**, until you reach 69th Street.

6. Last, you make a **left / right** turn, going **south / north** onto 69th Street.

STUDY SKILL: Interpret traffic signs

Match each traffic sign with the correct meaning in the box. Write the letters.

____ 1.    ____ 2.    ____ 3.    ____ 4.

____ 5.    ____ 6.   ____ 7.   ____ 8.

a. Stay right of median

b. High-occupancy vehicle lane; only for cars with two or more persons

c. Railroad crossing

d. Left turn only; you may not continue straight in this lane

e. U.S. numbered route

f. You may not cross over the dividing line in order to pass other cars

g. You must let other traffic go first when you see this sign

h. Alternative route you can take when there is road construction

A Read the letter to the editor. Circle the four topic sentences in the paragraphs. Then cross out any details that do not relate to the topic or do not support the writer's argument. The first one is done for you. Find four more.

Letter to the Editor:

People should not use cell phones while driving. ~~Everyone I know has a cell phone.~~ To be good drivers, people must observe and concentrate. People who talk on cell phones while driving are not paying attention to the road. This inattention causes many accidents each year.

There is a lot of evidence that using a cell phone while driving is reckless and dangerous. A recent study by the Center for Driving Safety found that drivers using cell phones have the same kinds of accidents as drivers who are drunk. Of course, drinking while driving is not a very good idea, either. The study measured how a driver's attention is affected by talking on the phone. It found that just *listening* to a phone conversation consumes 37 percent of a person's attention span—enough to cause a person to weave into another lane without realizing it. The drivers in the study—two of them were women—were from Fresno, California.

Cell phones, both hand-held and hands-free, are equally dangerous. The study concluded that hands-free devices, such as cell phone speakers, do not reduce accidents. A person talking on a cell phone is paying attention to the conversation whether he or she is holding the phone or not. Sometimes I think people should not be allowed to listen to the radio or talk while driving, either.

Driving requires responsible behavior. Using cell phones while driving can result in serious accidents so drivers must refrain from using them. Cell phone use by drivers also needs to be outlawed in every state.

B Answer the questions.

1. What is the writer's main argument?

   _____

2. What is one statistic the writer gives to support his argument?

   _____

3. What does the writer think about the use of hands-free phones while driving?

   _____

Review and Expand: Vocabulary

A Match the words with their definitions. Write the letters.

_____ 1. display   a. tools and machines you need for a particular activity

_____ 2. distracted   b. people who work in a company or for an employer

_____ 3. equipment   c. unable to pay attention to what you are doing

_____ 4. interior   d. part of a machine that shows information

_____ 5. personnel   e. skilled, trained, or expert at something

_____ 6. professional   f. inner part or inside of something

B Complete the sentences with words from Exercise A.

1. The car's _____ included a global positioning device and leather seats.

2. The mechanic used special _____ to fix the car engine.

3. We consulted a _____ salesperson about what type of insurance we needed.

4. Many drivers become _____ if they try to eat and drive at the same time.

C Read the sentences. Underline the synonym clues that help you understand the boldface word.

1. Jenny publishes a newspaper about our company's **personnel**. The newspaper contains articles about the company's workers.

2. What kinds of **equipment**, or tools, do you keep in the trunk of your car in case you have car trouble?

3. When I need to get somewhere quickly, I take roads for fast traffic, such as the **interstate**.

4. My **registration** and other official documents about my car are in the glove compartment.

> **Learning Strategy:**
> Using synonym clues
>
> When you come across an unfamiliar word, look for context clues, such as synonyms, in the surrounding words and sentences. Synonyms are words with the same or nearly the same meanings. Often words or phrases near the unfamiliar word have a similar meaning.

READ

Read the article. As you read, summarize parts of the text. Write the important ideas in your notebook.

> **Reading Skill:**
> Summarizing
>
> As you read, stop to summarize parts of a text so that you will remember and understand what you read. Write a few sentences about the main ideas. Leave out unimportant events, ideas, and details. When you finish reading, summarize the entire text.

Thunder and Lightning

Thunderstorms occur all over the world. Thunder and lightning usually accompany thunderstorms. Lightning is an electrical discharge that can travel 60,000 miles per second and can be five times hotter than the surface of the sun. Thunder is the sound made by lightning. Thunderstorms can be severe and cause damage. Take these steps to be safe.

If a thunderstorm is predicted for your area, first bring inside objects that could blow away in strong winds. For example, bring in trash or recycling bins. Next, make sure items in your home are safe. Unplug electrical items such as appliances and computers. Power surges from lightning can damage these items. Once a thunderstorm starts, follow the 30/30 rule. When you first see lightning, count to 30. If you hear thunder before you reach 30, go indoors. Stay in the basement or in the room with the fewest windows. Stay inside 30 minutes after you hear the last thunderclap. If you are in a vehicle, try to get inside the nearest building. If you are not able to do this, stay in your vehicle.

Fact or Fiction?

- Lightning never strikes twice in the same place.

  FICTION. *Lightning often strikes the same place more than once.*

- Taking a shower or bath during a thunderstorm is dangerous.

  FACT. *Pipes can conduct electricity if lightning hits your home.*

- Talking on the phone during a thunderstorm can be dangerous.

  FACT AND FICTION. *This is only true for phones that have a cord. It's safe to use cordless phones and cell phones.*

- Shoes with rubber soles and rubber tires protect you from lightning.

  FICTION. *A small amount of rubber does not protect you when lightning strikes.*

- Never touch someone who has been hit by lightning.

  FICTION. *It's safe to touch people hit by lightning and important to do so if they need first aid. 90 percent of people hit by lightning survive.*

CHECK YOUR UNDERSTANDING

A Read the article again. Match each summary with the correct paragraph of the article. Write (paragraph) *1* or *2*.

_____ There are many things you can do to say safe when there is a thunderstorm. You should secure items in your home and outside. Stay inside or in your vehicle until the thunderstorm is over.

_____ Thunderstorms involve thunder and lightning and can cause damage. Lightning is an electrical discharge, and thunder is a sound made by lightning.

B Read the statements. Write *T* (true) or *F* (false).

_F_ 1. Thunder is an electrical discharge.

_____ 2. Lightning can travel 100,000 miles an hour.

_____ 3. You should bring items inside that could blow away in a thunderstorm.

_____ 4. Power surges can damage computers.

_____ 5. You should stay indoors one hour after you hear the last thunderclap in a storm.

_____ 6. You should never stay in your vehicle during a thunderstorm.

_____ 7. Lightning can strike in the same place more than once.

_____ 8. It's safe to use a cell phone during a thunderstorm.

_____ 9. Shoes with rubber soles protect you from lightning.

_____ 10. Most people die after lightning hits them.

C Answer the questions.

1. What is the 30/30 rule?

_____

_____

2. Why is it dangerous to take a shower or bath during a thunderstorm?

_____

_____

A Change the passive sentences to active sentences.

1. The workers might have been hurt by the accident.

   The accident might have hurt the workers.

2. Many houses could have been destroyed by the hurricane.

   _____

3. The building should have been evacuated by the fire chief.

   _____

4. The town should have been warned by the police.

   _____

5. The trash cans should have been collected by the building manager.

   _____

B Complete the sentences.

1. Tanya didn't evacuate her home during the flood. She had to wait for help. She should

   _____have evacuated_____. She shouldn't _____have stayed home_____.

2. Ernesto didn't watch the news on Friday. He didn't know there was going to be an

   earthquake. He went to work. He should _____. He

   shouldn't _____.

3. The police warned Ai-Lun to lock her doors at night, but she didn't listen. She didn't lock

   them. She was lucky. She wasn't robbed. She should _____. She

   might _____.

4. Jordan and Solomon didn't prepare an emergency kit for their home. The lights went out,

   and they didn't have a flashlight or candle. They had to sit in the dark for five hours. They

   should _____. They might not _____.

C Complete the conversation. Circle the correct words.

Linh: Hi, Jesse. Did you hear about the hurricane in Florida?

Jesse: Yes, I did. My aunt and uncle live in Miami.

Linh: Wow! Are they OK?

Jesse: Yes, they are. But it was a bad situation because they stayed for a while. They didn't realize that the hurricane would be so dangerous. If they had known that, they **might not have been** / **might not have** stayed.

Linh: Wasn't there a warning on the news? They **should have been** / **should have** warned right away.

Jesse: No, at first there was no warning to evacuate. Later the governor went on TV and gave the evacuation order.

Linh: So, did they evacuate then?

Jesse: Not at first. They **should have been** / **should have** evacuated right away, but they didn't. At last, my mother called them and convinced them. They **might not have been** / **might not have** left otherwise. It was a good thing she did because their home was badly damaged. They **could have been** / **could have** hurt.

Linh: It's a good thing that they left. Miami got hit very badly. The city **should have been** / **should have** more prepared for the hurricane.

D MAKE IT PERSONAL. Complete the sentences with your own opinions.

You were in your car. You turned on the radio and heard there was a thunderstorm. You parked your car in a parking lot and sat under a tree for protection. Lightning hit a tree near you. You were very lucky.

1. You could have _____.

2. You might not have _____.

3. You should have _____.

4. You shouldn't have _____.

DICTIONARY SKILL: Finding the right meaning

Many English words have more than one meaning. When a dictionary entry has more than one meaning, you will see a number (*1, 2, 3*, etc.) before each meaning or *definition*. The first meaning is the most common one. Look at the example.

> **haz•ard**[1] /ˈhæzəd/ *n.* [C] **1** something that may be dangerous or cause accidents, problems, etc.: *a health hazard* | *the hazards of starting your own business*
> **2 occupational hazard** a problem or risk that cannot be avoided in the job that you do—**hazardous** *adj.*: *hazardous waste from factories*

Read each pair of definitions and sentences. Complete each pair with one word in the box. Check your answers in a dictionary.

> disaster   flood   safe   uproot

1. Not likely to cause or allow any physical injury or harm: *Have a* _____ *trip.*

   Not involving any risk and very likely to succeed: *U.S. Treasury bonds are considered a* _____ *investment.*

2. To pull a plant and its roots out of the ground: *The elephant's trunk is powerful enough to* _____ *trees.*

   To force a person or people to leave a home or homeland and move to a different place: *Because of the war in Kosovo, Genti had to* _____ *his family and move to the United States.*

3. A sudden event such as a hurricane that causes great harm or damage: *Hurricane Katrina was a terrible natural* _____ .

   A complete failure: *The party was a total* _____! *The food was terrible and the music was too loud.*

4. A very large amount of water that covers an area that is usually dry: *The* _____ *was caused by the storm, which brought a huge amount of rain.*

   A very large number of things or people that arrive at the same time: *The TV station has received a* _____ *of complaints about last night's show.*

WORD STUDY: Understanding word families

Most English words belong to a word "family." These words all have related meanings but different forms of speech. For example, *rotate* (verb), *rotation* (noun), and *rotating* (adjective) all belong to a word family. They all describe turning in a circle around a fixed point.

A Complete the chart of word families. Write the missing words and check your answers in a dictionary. More than one form is sometimes possible for some parts of speech. If a part of speech does not exist for that word, write *X*.

Verb	Noun	Adjective
center	center	
confide	confidence	
damage		damaged damaging
discriminate		discriminating
prevent		
	safe safety	safe
survive		surviving
trap	trap	

B Complete each sentence with the correct part of speech of the word in parentheses. Use the word families chart above as a guide.

1. "Tornado Alley" is located in the _____central_____ (center) part of the United States.

2. She asked her coworker not to discuss the matter with anyone. She wanted to keep it _____ (confide).

3. The flood caused a huge amount of _____ (damage) to their property.

4. The law prohibits _____ (discriminate) against people on the basis of race, religion, sex, or age. This means that it is against the law to treat people unfairly because of their race, religion, sex, or age.

5. OSHA is an organization that sets standards for the _____ (prevent) of unsafe and unhealthful situations in the workplace.

6. If you want to _____ (survive) a powerful hurricane, it is important to have a good emergency plan.

7. The woman was rescued after eight days of being _____ (trap) in the rubble.

LIFE SKILLS

A Match the words in the box to the pictures. Write the words.

> hand brakes   helmet   reflectors   sewer grate

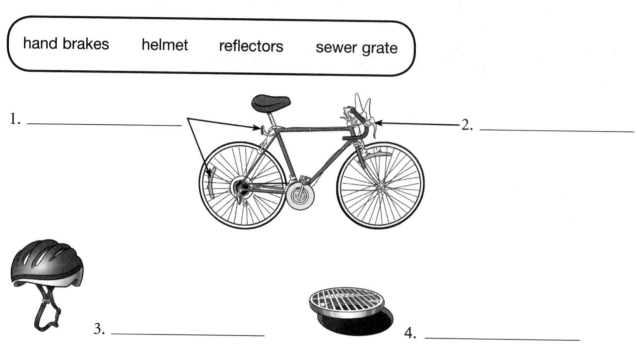

1. _____

2. _____

3. _____

4. _____

B Read the safety poster. What is the topic?

BICYCLE SAFETY IS NO ACCIDENT

Bicycle accidents kill 900 people every year, and send about 567,000 to hospital emergency rooms with injuries. Studies have shown that helmet use reduces injuries by 85 percent. Follow these rules when you ride:

- Always wear a helmet to help prevent head injuries.
- Observe all traffic laws and signals, just as cars must do.
- Don't ride double (with two people) on a bicycle.
- Ride near the curb and in the same direction as traffic.
- Find alternate routes rather than ride through busy intersections or through heavy or high-speed traffic. Always look out for traffic.

- Walk—don't ride—your bicycle across busy intersections and left-turn corners.
- Avoid riding in wet weather. When the road is wet, handbrakes may require a longer distance to stop.
- Avoid riding in the dark. If you do, be sure the bike is equipped with a headlight, a taillight, and reflectors. Wear light colors and reflective vests and jackets.
- Avoid loose clothing or long coats that can catch in pedals or wheels.
- Avoid crossing raised sewer grates.

C Read the statements about the safety poster. Write *T* (true) or *F* (false).

_____ 1. If you ride a bicycle at night, you should wear special clothing so drivers can see you.

_____ 2. It is safe to ride over a sewer grate on a bicycle if you ride slowly.

_____ 3. If you wear a bicycle helmet, there is a much greater chance that you will not get a head injury in an accident.

_____ 4. When you ride a bicycle in wet weather, the brakes work faster than they usually do.

_____ 5. If you see a stoplight, it is OK to ride through it on a bicycle if you do not see any car coming within 50 feet.

_____ 6. When you ride a bicycle, you should ride with the traffic facing you so that you can see oncoming cars.

STUDY SKILL: Read a pie chart and a bar graph

Read the charts that show children's use of helmets. Answer the questions.

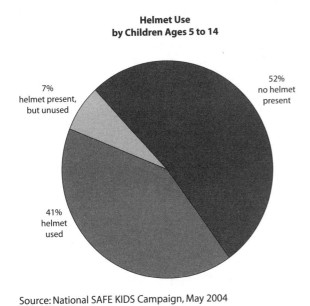

Helmet Use
by Children Ages 5 to 14

52% no helmet present

7% helmet present, but unused

41% helmet used

Source: National SAFE KIDS Campaign, May 2004

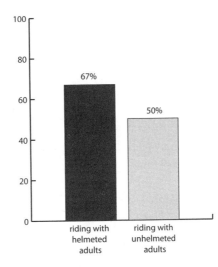

Helmet Use of Children Ages 5 to 14
by Helmet Use of Adult Companions

67% riding with helmeted adults

50% riding with unhelmeted adults

1. What percentage of children did not have a helmet? _____

2. What percentage of children had a helmet but did not use it? _____

3. What does the study about children and adults show? _____
   a. When children ride with adults, more children wear helmets.
   b. When children ride with adults, fewer children wear helmets.
   c. Children are not influenced by adult companions.

READ

Read the article. Highlight the common workplace injuries and illnesses.

Reading Skill:
Monitoring comprehension

Monitoring your comprehension will help you understand difficult texts, such as government documents. Reread such texts slowly and carefully. List any difficult words. Try to figure out their meanings from clues in the surrounding words and sentences. If you can't figure out a word, look it up in a dictionary. Then try to restate the information in your own words.

INJURIES AND ILLNESSES

Workplace injuries and illnesses are a problem for many people. Statistics show that in the United States, accidents and illnesses happen most frequently in mid-size companies (50 to 249 employees). Approximately 50 percent of all injuries and illnesses result in employees missing work. Listed below are some common injuries and illnesses.

Slips and Trips

Many accidents happen each year when employees trip over objects in the workplace. These are usually items put in places they shouldn't be. Slipping on wet floors also causes many injuries. This type of injury can happen in any work setting.

Sprains and Strains

A lot of people sprain or strain muscles at work. These types of injuries are usually caused by manual labor such as lifting, pushing, pulling, or carrying heavy objects. These injuries occur most commonly in warehouses.

Shocks

Electrical equipment can cause shocks. Only licensed electricians should ever touch equipment that can have an electrical discharge. Dangerous equipment needs to be labeled with signs that indicate shock or voltage.

Hearing Loss

Hearing loss is a common workplace injury in jobs where people are exposed to extremely loud noises over an extended period. People who work in factories often have hearing loss. Because of new safety regulations, the number of people suffering hearing loss has been decreasing every year.

Carcinogens

Carcinogens are substances that cause cancer. Asbestos is a well-known carcinogen. This material is sometimes put behind walls or above ceilings to fireproof or insulate buildings. It isn't used anymore, but it is still present in many older buildings. Workers can develop lung cancer from breathing in asbestos. People who work in an environment with asbestos or other carcinogens need to wear protective respiratory equipment.

Other Biohazards

In addition to cancer-causing materials, work sites may have other substances that are biological hazards. For example, hospitals have many biohazards from sick patients. These substances carry microorganisms that could give workers viral infections such as rubella or tuberculosis. Workers need to handle biohazardous materials carefully and dispose of them safely.

CHECK YOUR UNDERSTANDING

A Match the signs with the headings in the article.

1. _____

2. _____

3. _____

4. _____

5. _____

6. _____

B Read the statements. Write *T* (true) or *F* (false).

_____ 1. Asbestos is a material that can cause cancer.

_____ 2. Construction workers may be exposed to asbestos.

_____ 3. Biohazards can cause viruses, infections, or other illnesses.

_____ 4. Slips and trips usually only happen in office buildings or factories.

_____ 5. More workers are suffering hearing loss now than they did in the past.

C Match the words from the article with the definitions. Write the letters.

1. _____ occur

2. _____ manual labor

3. _____ hazardous substances

4. _____ extended period

a. dangerous materials

b. happen

c. a long time

d. work done by hand, without machines

LIFE SKILLS

Look at the chart showing workplace injuries and illnesses. Circle the correct answers.

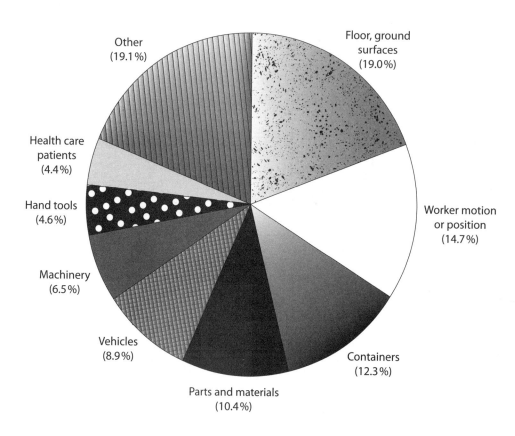

1. According to the chart, which of these results in more accidents?

   a. parts and materials   b. worker motion or position   c. containers

2. What percentage of accidents is caused by floor and ground surfaces?

   a. 19   b. 14.7   c. 19.1

3. What category has the lowest number of illnesses and accidents?

   a. hand tools   b. health care patients   c. machinery

4. What percentage of accidents is caused in health care settings?

   a. 10.4   b. 14.7   c. 4.4

STUDY SKILL: Make inferences

Read about the workplaces. What is the health hazard in each one? Write the correct words in the box.

> chemical hazard   electrical hazard   excessive noise
> extreme temperatures   worker motion or position

1. Javier is an exterminator who sprays pesticides in people's homes to kill insects. Recently, he has been having trouble breathing. He coughs a lot, and he sometimes has headaches.

   _____

2. Lin works in a meatpacking factory. The machines are very loud. She has noticed that she often cannot hear people.

   _____

3. Sam works in the boiler room of a large company. Recently, he has been having sweaty palms, his safety glasses fog up, and he feels dizzy.

   _____

4. Anna is a medical claims processor. She works on the computer all day, and her job involves a lot of typing. Lately she has been getting shooting pains in her right hand and arm.

   _____

5. Ming works as a florist in a small garden center. There are extensions cords all over the floor. Yesterday, when she plugged in the fan by her desk, there was a crackling noise and smoke came out of the electrical outlet.

   _____

READ

Read about fire safety. Underline the imperatives. Circle any signal words.

How to Prevent Fires in the Home

The Home Safety Council reports that fires and burns are the third leading cause of unintentional injury and related deaths in the home. Most of these fires could be prevented. For example, some fires have started when people smoked at home and did not extinguish the cigarette. Follow these safety tips to reduce the chance of fire in your home.

First, identify the most common sources of fires in the home. Many fires start in the kitchen. Do not leave the room when you are cooking. If you must leave, then turn off the stove. Make sure that all flammable materials, such as towels and oven mitts, are kept away from the stove. You should not wear loose clothing when cooking.

Electrical appliances and cords also cause fires. If an appliance overheats or sparks, turn it off immediately and unplug it. It's important to replace the appliance or to have it professionally repaired. Extension cords should only be used on a temporary basis. Do not place electrical cords under rugs or in areas where people walk. Cover unused outlets with safety caps, especially if there are small children in the home.

Candles should be used with care. Never place candles near something that could burn. Blow out all candles when you leave a room. Do not use candles in bedrooms or other areas where people sleep.

After you have identified potential hazards, the next step is to install alarm systems. Make sure every floor of the home and every bedroom has a smoke alarm. Test the alarms once a month to be certain they're working. Also, consider installing a home sprinkler system. Sprinklers greatly increase your chances of surviving a home fire.

Finally, have an escape plan. Try to have two escape routes from every room. Practice your escape plans with your family at least once a month. These simple precautions can save your life and the lives of your family members.

A Match the words with their definitions. Write the letters.

_____ 1. furnish

_____ 2. toxic

_____ 3. comply

_____ 4. sturdy

_____ 5. substance

a. strong and not likely to break or be hurt

b. supply or provide something

c. a particular type of solid, liquid, or gas

d. poisonous

e. do what you are asked to do or what a law or rule tells you to do

B Use the words in Exercise A to complete the sentences.

1. Residents were asked to _____ with the evacuation order because the city was in the direct path of the hurricane.

2. It is important to keep _____ liquids in tightly sealed containers and out of reach of small children.

3. The Red Cross will _____ everyone in the emergency shelter with a blanket and other necessities.

4. After the storm, the fish in the river were covered with a dark, oily _____.

5. Although the building looked _____, it collapsed during the earthquake.

C Make vocabulary cards for the words *substance* and *toxic*. For each word, include one expression that uses the word.

Learning Strategy:
Expressions with key vocabulary

Recording expressions that use key vocabulary is a good way to learn the vocabulary. For example, a **health hazard** is something that poses a threat to your health.

READ

Read the web page. Circle the main idea.

a. Asking for more responsibility is a good idea.

b. It's important to take initiative at work.

c. If you see something that needs to be done, do it.

🗙 ⊖ ⊕

http://www.workhelp.com

Time to Take Initiative

When you are at work, you don't always have to wait for your supervisor to tell you what to do. Taking initiative at work is important. It can not only lead to promotion, but also make the job more rewarding for you. Here are some ways you can take initiative at work.

Do It!

If you see something that needs to be done . . . *just do it*! Perhaps you see papers that need to be filed. Don't wait for someone else to take care of them.

> *Tip:* Make sure you are not doing something that someone else was supposed to do. The goal is to improve yourself and help the company, not to get someone else in trouble!

Say It.

Don't be afraid to give your opinion when you are asked to. A supervisor might ask for your opinion in a private meeting or in a group meeting. Say what you think about problems and solutions.

> *Tip:* Be sure to express your opinions in a positive way. Also remember that someone may listen to your opinion, but not always follow it. Be ready to follow company decisions even if they don't always match your suggestions and ideas.

Ask for It.

Perhaps you don't feel challenged at work. Ask your supervisor for more responsibilities. Supervisors are usually impressed by people who want to work beyond the expectations of the position.

> *Tip:* Don't take on more than you can handle. Make sure you are successfully meeting the responsibilities that go with your position before you ask for more.

CHECK YOUR UNDERSTANDING

A Read the article again. Check *Do* or *Don't*.

	Do	Don't
1. Take initiative to improve things at work.	✓	
2. Do things at work that might get someone else in trouble.		✓
3. Give your opinion when your supervisor asks for it.		✓
4. Give your opinions in a firm way even if you sound negative.		✓
5. Ask for more work than you can finish.	✓	
6. Try to work beyond the expectations of your position.	✓	
7. Meet your responsibilities before you ask for more work.	✓	

B Read the paragraphs. Did the employee *Do It, Say It,* or *Ask for It*?

1. _Do It_

   Barbara works at a Pro Office. She notices that some of her co-workers are having trouble with the English names of some of the supplies. She starts helping them learn the new words at lunchtime.

2. _Ask for it_

   Tuan volunteers at a library. He puts books back on the shelves. He always finishes early. He asks the librarian for more work. He is going to learn how to help people check out books tomorrow.

3. _Do it_

   Jarvas enters information into a computer at work every day. He doesn't think the system works very well. He makes some small changes to make the process easier. He teaches his co-workers how to use the new system.

4. _Say it_

   At a meeting, Mrs. Huang asks her employees how they can make the lines move faster at RightMart. Sahra suggests that they hire one more cashier and open one of the cash registers that isn't being used.

READ

Scan the article. Which time periods does it mention?

a. before and after a performance review

b. during a performance review

c. before, during, and after a performance review

Reading Skill:
Scanning

Scanning helps readers find specific information and key words in a text. Scan to answer a specific question or to decide whether a text contains information you need.

Performance Perfection

Some people think performance reviews are a waste of time. Many employees don't realize that performance reviews can be very useful. Make the most of your performance review. Follow these tips:

First, prepare for the performance review. If you work for a company, find out when you are going to have the performance review. If you work for a smaller company, your boss may not normally give a performance review. You can ask for one. Then prepare for the review. It is a good idea to prepare one month beforehand. Look over your goals from last year. Did you meet them? Write a self-evaluation. Sometimes the company gives employees this form to fill out. If they don't, write one for yourself. In your self-evaluation, write your strengths, the goals you accomplished, and the areas you think you need to improve in.

Next comes the review itself. Performance reviews give you a chance to communicate with your manager. Tell your manager how you are important to the team. Ask questions about anything you don't understand and tell your supervisor if there is a rating you don't agree with. During the review, offer suggestions on how you could improve. Most important, make sure you understand the goals and objectives set for the next performance review. When your review is over, you should have some new insights, for example, information about the company, your job description, your team's goals, or your manager's likes and dislikes.

Afterward, safely file your performance review somewhere easy to locate. Occasionally look at your review and see how you are doing in areas that might have been weak. Be sure you are continuing to be strong in areas where you've done well. You can use your review to periodically check your progress and to make sure you are meeting goals and objectives. This will insure you have stayed on track or improved before your next review.

Good reviews can be useful in the future. If you are asking for a promotion, you can use a good review to remind your supervisor how well you are doing. You can also use reviews when applying for other jobs. Save your reviews for at least five years. They might be useful long after you've left a job.

CHECK YOUR UNDERSTANDING

A Read the article again. Write *B* for before a performance review, *D* for during a performance review, or *A* for after.

_D_ 1. Tell your supervisor if you don't agree with something on the review.

____ 2. Show your review to an employer during a job interview.

____ 3. Ask your supervisor about something you don't understand.

____ 4. Look over your goals from last year.

____ 5. Look at your review and make sure you are on the right track.

____ 6. Make sure you understand your goals and objectives for the coming year.

____ 7. Write a self-evaluation.

B Read the questions. Circle the correct answers.

1. How early should you prepare for your review?

   a. a week before   b. a month before

2. What should you suggest during your next review?

   a. ways you can improve   b. goals for the company

3. How long should you save your review after your evaluation?

   a. five months   b. five years

C Read the statements. Write *T* (true), *F* (false), or *D* (doesn't say).

_D_ 1. All performance reviews have ratings.

____ 2. It's a good idea to offer suggestions during your review.

____ 3. Do not express disagreement with a rating.

____ 4. When you look back at your review, you should only pay attention to the areas where you need improvement.

____ 5. A good review doesn't help you to get a promotion.

A Check (✓) if the sentences in each pair have the same meaning. If they do not, rewrite the second sentence to match the first.

_____ 1. Michal can't speak Spanish, but he can speak Portuguese.

Michal can't speak Spanish unless he can speak Portuguese.

Michal can't speak Spanish although he can speak Portuguese.

_____ 2. Annette is going to quit her job if she doesn't get a promotion.

Annette is going to quit her job unless she gets a promotion.

_____ 3. I'm going to save my performance evaluation even though it wasn't very good.

I'm going to save my performance evaluation, although it wasn't very good.

_____ 4. Hai did very well at the interview, but he didn't make eye contact.

Hai won't do well at the interview unless he makes eye contact.

_____ 5. Susan can only go to the interview on Tuesday if she gets a babysitter.

Susan will go to the interview on Tuesday although she doesn't have a babysitter.

B Complete each sentence with *although* or *unless.*

1. Marjorie won't get a promotion _____unless_____ she takes more initiative.

2. _____ Clayton pays attention, he never remembers what was said.

3. Ms. Torres usually isn't very efficient _____ she does do payroll quickly.

4. Soo-Jin won't get a promotion _____ she works harder.

5. _____ Mr. Wilson follows OSHA guidelines, there will be an accident.

6. Martin got the job _____ he wasn't qualified for it.

C Write sentences with *although* or *unless.* Write the sentences two ways.

1. Tabitha / improve / her computer skills / not / get a job (unless)

   Unless Tabitha improves her computer skills, she won't get a job.

   Tabitha won't get a job unless she improves her computer skills.

2. Miranda / not / take criticism well / listen / to Mrs. Addison (although)

   _____

   _____

3. Mr. Yeom / be / a good supervisor / have / a bad temper (although)

   _____

   _____

4. Cynthia / get to work on time / miss / the bus (unless)

   _____

   _____

LIFE SKILLS

A Read about apprenticeships.

The State of California, together with employers, offers apprenticeship programs in many skilled occupations. Apprentices get both on-the-job and classroom training for a period of one to six years. They are paid a percentage of the skilled worker's wage to start, and then they receive regular pay increases. When they graduate, they get a certificate of completion from the State of California.

B Look at the chart about apprenticeship programs. Which programs last the longest? Which program is the shortest?

Trade or occupation:	Air conditioning mechanic	Maintenance plumber	Firefighter	Vocational nurse
Program length:	60 months	60 months	36 months	24 months
Starting wage:	$14.28/hr.	50% of journeyman's wages	Varies by department	40% to 60% of voc. nurse wages
Minimum age:	18	18	18	18
Education prerequisites:	High School Graduation or GED or Equivalent	High School Graduation or GED or Equivalent	High School Graduation or GED or Equivalent	High School Graduation or GED or Equivalent
Additional prerequisites:	None	Must be able to read, write, and speak English	Pass physical dexterity test	C.N.A. State Certificate or documentation of current employment for minimum of six (6) months as a C.N.A.
Exams:	Written Test: Yes Oral Exam: Yes	Written Test: Yes Oral Exam: None	Written Test: Yes Oral Exam: Yes	Written Test: Yes Oral Exam: Yes
Additional requirements:	None	Must be physically able to perform all work of the occupation	To be a successful firefighter, a candidate must be both physically and mentally fit, and must have the ability to function as a team player.	None
Contact information:	**Bay Area Sheet Metal J.A.C.** 1700 Marina Blvd. San Leandro, CA 94577	**Kern, Inyo & Mono Counties Plumbing, Pipefitter & Refrigeration/ Air Conditioning Mechanic J.A.T.C.** 6820 Meany Ave Bakersfield, CA 93308	**California Fire Fighter Joint Apprenticeship Committee** www.cffjac.org 1780 Creekside Oaks Drive #201 Sacramento, CA 95833	**Clovis Adult School Nursing Program** 1452 David E. Cook Way Clovis, CA 93611
Applications taken:	San Francisco Sheetmetal JATC. 1939 Market Street, San Francisco, CA	Applications taken every Monday between 9:00 A.M. and 11:00 A.M.		Contact the above location for existing placement possibilities.

STUDY SKILL: Interpret a chart

Answer the questions about the chart.

1. How long is the program for the maintenance plumber?

   _____

2. How long is the firefighter program?

   _____

3. What is the starting hourly wage for an air conditioning mechanic?

   _____

4. How old must you be for all the programs?

   _____

5. What are the education requirements for all?

   _____

6. Which program does not include an oral exam?

   _____

7. Which programs have additional prerequisites?

   _____

8. Which job requires certification?

   _____

9. Which two jobs are the most physically demanding?

   _____

10. Which program lists the hours that applications are taken?

   _____

DICTIONARY SKILL: Locating word forms

Use your dictionary to learn more about the different members of a word family. Some word forms have their own entries in a dictionary. Others word forms may appear within a main entry for the base word. For example, *adaptability* appears at the end of the entry for *adaptable*.

a•dapt /əˈdæpt/ *v.* **1** [I,T] to change your behavior or ideas to fit a new situation: *The kids are having trouble adapting to their new school.* | *These plants are able to adapt themselves to desert conditions.* **2** [T] to change something so that it is appropriate for a new purpose: *The car has been adapted to take unleaded gas.* | *The house was adapted for wheelchair users.*
a•dapt•a•ble /əˈdæptəbəl/ *adj.* able to change and be successful in new and different situations—**adaptability** /əˈdæpˈtəbɪlət̬i/ *n.* [U]
ad•ap•ta•tion /ˌædəpˈteɪʃən, ædæp-/ *n.* **1** [C] a play, film, or television program that is based on a book **2** [U] the process of changing something so that it can be used in a different way or in different conditions

di•verse /dəˈvɚs, daɪ-/ *adj.* very different from each other: *The U.S. is a culturally diverse nation.*
di•ver•si•fy /dəˈvɚsəˌfaɪ, daɪ-/ *v.* (**diversified, diversifies**) [I,T] if a company diversifies, it begins to make new types of products or to become involved in new types of business in addition to what it already does: *They started as a cosmetics company and then diversified into clothing. The company needs to diversify its products.* —diversification /dəˈvɚsəfəˈkeɪʃən/ *n.* [U]

di•ver•si•ty /dəˈvɚsət̬i, daɪ-/ *n.* [singular, U] a range of different people or things [= **variety**]: *The school prides itself on its ethnic/diversity.* | *a diversity of opinions*

Use the dictionary entries above to complete the word family chart for *adapt* and *diverse*.

Key word	Verbs	Nouns	Adjectives
adapt	(adapt)	1. adaptability 2.	
diverse		1. 2.	(diverse)

WORD STUDY: Learning idioms

A Read the sentences and definitions for common workplace idioms below.

1. I was surprised when my supervisor told me **out of the blue** that I was receiving a promotion.

> **out of the blue** = in a surprising way; without any reason to expect it

2. It's going **to cost** the company **an arm and a leg** to rent new office space.

> **to cost an arm and a leg** = to cost a lot; be expensive

3. Do you have this new computer program **down pat**?

> **down pat** = know it so well that you can do it without having to think about it

4. The job requires someone who can **hit the ground running**.

> **hit the ground running** = start a new job or position in a speedy, competent way

5. My co-worker and I get along well; we **see eye to eye** on many issues.

> **see eye to eye** = agree

B Write a sentence of your own for each of the idioms above.

1. _____

2. _____

3. _____

4. _____

5. _____

Read the self-evaluation. The writer is trying to show that he is a good EMT. Cross out the example sentences that do not give good support.

Medical City Dallas Hospital
2010 Employee Self-Appraisal
Employee Comments (page 4):
In the space below, please comment on your job strengths and accomplishments.

Self-Evaluation

I have been working for Mercy Hospital as an emergency medical technician (EMT) for one year. I think I have done an excellent job.

I have shown that I have a number of strengths that are important for an EMT. One of my strengths is that I am always very careful. For example, as an ambulance driver, I have only been in two accidents. In both of those accidents, I fell asleep behind the wheel. Also, I take careful notes. I always take the time to make careful notes about the accident, the patient, and the treatment we administered. The hospital admitting staff has criticized my notes numerous times for bad handwriting, but I am working on this.

In the past year, I have improved my ability to assess an emergency situation and deliver the appropriate care. Several of the ER doctors have commented that I have done a good job assisting the patients. However, a month ago I administered CPR incorrectly to a woman and injured her. I was tired from working overtime.

Another of my strengths is my ability to communicate well. I reassure patients and make them feel comfortable. Several patients have complained that I did not answer their questions. It's important to me for patients to have confidence in the emergency technicians, and I try to answer their questions.

For my future goals, there are certain areas in which I could do better. I would like to learn more about certain medical equipment, such as ventilators. I have a number of goals for myself for the next year. I would also like to take a course in dealing with traffic jams.

A Match the words with their definitions. Write the letters.

_____ 1. adjust   a. able to change easily

_____ 2. concentrate   b. one of several things that influence or cause a situation

_____ 3. factor   c. gradually become familiar with a new situation

_____ 4. flexible   d. think very carefully about something you are doing

B Use the words in Exercise A to complete the sentences.

1. Iris had to _____ to a new situation when she was promoted.

2. Her supervisor asked her to _____ on learning a new system.

3. Iris is a very _____ person, so she adapted easily to her new job.

4. Iris's ability to hit the ground running was a major _____ in her success.

C Study this vocabulary card made by a Polish student for the word *flexible*. Then make cards for the words in Exercise A. Follow the model. Include keywords.

> **Learning Strategy:**
> Using the keyword method
>
> The keyword method can help you learn and remember new words. It involves associating a new word with a known word and a picture.

First language translation for *flexible*: elastyczny (in Polish)	Keyword: rubber band
Second language definition 1. able to change easily 2. able to bend or be bent easily	Memory and Meaning Link Rubber bands remind me of the word *flexible* because they stretch.

DICTIONARY SKILL: Using phonetic spellings and pronunciation tables

Dictionaries provide a pronunciation table at the beginning of the book that explains the sound of each phonetic symbol.

Study the pronunciation table from the *Longman Dictionary of American English (LDAE).* Then use the pronunciation table to match the words with their phonetic spellings.

  _c_   1. bridge

____ 2. cholesterol

____ 3. embarrassed

____ 4. inhale

____ 5. specialist

____ 6. symptom

---

a. ɪnˈheɪl

b. ˈsɪmptəm

c. brɪdʒ

d. ˈspɛʃəlɪst

e. ɪmˈbærəst

f. kəˈlɛstəˌrɔl

Pronunciation Table

Vowels		Consonants	
Symbol	Key Word	Symbol	Key Word
i	beat, feed	p	pack, happy
ɪ	bit, did	b	back, rubber
eɪ	date, paid	t	tie
ɛ	bet, bed	d	die
æ	bat, bad	k	came, key, quick
ɑ	box, odd, father	g	game, guest
ɔ	bought, dog	tʃ	church, nature, watch
oʊ	boat, road	dʒ	judge, general, major
ʊ	book, good	f	fan, photograph
u	boot, food, student	v	van
ʌ	but, mud, mother	θ	thing, breath
ə	banana, among	ð	then, breathe
ɚ	shirt, murder	s	sip, city, psychology
aɪ	bite, cry, buy, eye	z	zip, please, goes
aʊ	about, how	ʃ	ship, machine, station,
ɔɪ	voice, boy		special, discussion
ɪr	beer	ʒ	measure, vision
ɛr	bare	h	hot, who
ɑr	bar	m	men, some
ɔr	door	n	sun, know, pneumonia
ʊr	tour	ŋ	sung, ringing
		w	wet, white
		l	light, long
		r	right, wrong
		y	yes, use, music
		t̬	butter, bottle
		tʰ	button

WORD STUDY: Understanding roots

In English, many of the words used to describe parts of the body come from Greek and Latin. Learning the meaning of common Greek and Latin roots will help you figure out the meanings of new words that contain those roots.

A Look at the chart. Notice the meaning of each root and the language it comes from. Then complete the chart. Use the words in the box below.

Root	Meaning	Original language	English words
manus	"hand"	Latin	1. *manicure* 2.
dens, dentis	"tooth"	Latin	3. 4.
pous, podos	"foot"	Greek	5. 6.
digitus	"finger"	Latin	7. 8.

dental   dentist   digit   digital

~~manicure~~   manually   octopus   podiatrist

B Write the word that fits each definition. Look at the chart for help.

1. a doctor who takes care of people's teeth _____*dentist*_____

2. a sea creature with eight legs _____

3. a doctor who takes care of people's feet _____

4. a treatment for the hands and fingernails _____

5. done with the hands _____

6. a written sign that represents any number from 0 to 9 _____

LIFE SKILLS

A Read the over-the-counter (OTC) *Drug Facts* label. Circle the active ingredient in the medicine.

Drug Facts

Active ingredient (in each tablet)   **Purpose**
Chlorpheniramine maleate 4 mg ....Antihistamine

Uses temporarily relieves those symptoms due to hay fever or other upper respiratory allergies: ■ sneezing   ■ runny nose   ■ itchy, watery eyes   ■ itchy throat

Warnings
Ask a doctor before use if you have
■ glaucoma   ■ a breathing problem such as emphysema or chronic bronchitis
■ trouble urinating due to an enlarged prostate gland

Ask a doctor or pharmacist before use if you are taking tranquilizers or sedatives

When using this product
■ you may get drowsy   ■ avoid alcoholic drinks
■ alcohol, sedatives, and tranquilizers may increase drowsiness
■ be careful when driving a motor vehicle or operating machinery
■ excitability may occur, especially in children

If pregnant or breast-feeding, ask a health professional before use.
Keep out of reach of children. In case of overdose, get medical help or contact a Posion Contol Center right away.

Directions

adults and children 12 years and over	take 1 tablet every 4 to 6 hours: not more than 6 tablets in 24 hours
children 6 years to under 12 years	take 1/2 tablet every 4 to 6 hours: not more than 3 tablets in 24 hours
children under 6 years	ask a doctor

Other Information ■ store at 20–25° C (68–77° F)   ■ protect from excessive moisture

Inactive ingredients DCS yellow no. 10, lactose, magnesium stearate, microcrystalline cellulose, pregelatinized starch

---

B Read the statements about the label. Write *T* (true) or *F* (false).

_____ 1. This medicine treats a runny nose.

_____ 2. Ask a doctor if you should use this medicine if you have a hearing problem.

_____ 3. The "When using this product" part of the label tells you when to take the medicine.

_____ 4. The maximum number of tablets a child 6 to 12 years old should take in 24 hours is 6.

_____ 5. The highest temperature you can store this medicine at is 68° F.

STUDY SKILL: Understand liquid measurements

When you take medicine or give it to a child, you need to measure the medicine exactly. Read the chart and answer the questions about dosages.

Many OTC (over-the-counter) medicines come with a measuring cup or syringe to take the medicine with.

Liquid Measurements

1 tablespoon (tbsp) = 3 teaspoons (tsp)

1 fl ounce (oz) = 2 tbsp

5 milliliters (mL) = 1 tsp

1 cubic centimeter (cc) = 1 mL

5 cc = 1 tsp

15 mL = 3 tsp

30 mL = 1 oz

---

1. You want to give your son 2 tbsp of cough medicine. How many teaspoons is this equal to? ___6___

2. The bottle of liquid aspirin says to give a ten-year-old child 5 cc. How many teaspoons is this? _____

3. How many milliliters are there in 1 tbsp? _____

4. How many ounces are there in 15 mL? _____

5. How many milliliters are there in 10 cc? _____

6. How many tablespoons are there in 2 oz? _____

READ

Read the article. Write the correct headings from the article under the pictures.

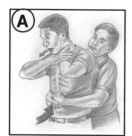 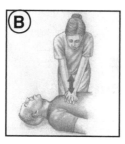 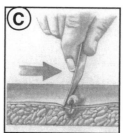

Reading Skill:
Visualizing

It is helpful to visualize, or form mental pictures, as you read. Use descriptive details in a text to picture the things, actions, or events you are reading about. This will help you to understand and remember information.

_____ _____ _____

First Aid Advice

It is a good idea to be prepared and to know what you should and shouldn't do in case of an emergency. Here are tips for administering first aid.

BITES

For minor insect or animal bites, wash the bite with soap and water. Put **antibiotic** cream on the bite, and cover it with a bandage. If the bite is bleeding a lot, if it is **infected**, or if you think the animal might have **rabies**, see a doctor immediately. For stings from insects like bees, scrape off the **stinger**, but do not pull it out, as this may cause the poison to spread. Put a cold cloth or ice pack on the wound. Take an **antihistamine** if needed to stop swelling. For serious reactions, call 911.

CHOKING

It is important to give first aid to someone who is choking right away. For adults and older children, hit the person on the back between the shoulder blades five times. Then perform the Heimlich maneuver. To do this, stand behind the person and put your arms around him or her. Lock your hands under the person's ribs, above the stomach. Push in five times quickly. This will dislodge the stuck object. It's important to do the Heimlich correctly. You can learn how in a training course. For infants, put the baby over your knee before giving five blows to the back. Instead of doing the Heimlich maneuver, use two fingers to press on the baby's chest.

CPR

CPR stands for cardiopulmonary resuscitation. This is a technique used when someone can't breathe or the heart has stopped. This technique involves pushing on the chest followed by mouth-to-mouth breathing. You can also take training courses in CPR. Only trained people should use both parts of the technique. If you are not trained, you can use the hand technique every two seconds on the chest until trained help arrives. Do not try the mouth-to-mouth breathing.

Source: www.mayoclinic.com/health/FirstAidIndex/FirstAidIndex

CHECK YOUR UNDERSTANDING

A Look at the boldfaced words from the article. Read the article again. Then match the words with their definitions. Write the letters.

_e_ 1. antibiotic

_____ 2. infected

_____ 3. rabies

_____ 4. antihistamine

_____ 5. stinger

a. a disease that animals sometimes get

b. a drug used to treat an allergic reaction

c. filled with harmful bacteria

d. a sharp, poisonous part of an insect

e. a drug used to kill bacteria and infections

B Read the statements. Write *T* (true) or *F* (false).

_F_ 1. You should put antibiotic cream on a bite before you wash it.

_____ 2. You should see a doctor if a bite is bleeding a lot.

_____ 3. Bee stingers contain poison.

_____ 4. You should wait for a doctor to give first aid to a choking person.

_____ 5. Stand in front of a person when doing the Heimlich maneuver.

_____ 6. When you help a choking infant, you should not do the Heimlich maneuver.

_____ 7. In CPR, push on the chest after you give mouth-to-mouth breathing.

_____ 8. If you aren't trained in CPR, don't use the hand technique.

C Correct the false statements in Exercise B.

You should put an antibiotic cream on a bite after you wash it.

_____

_____

_____

_____

_____

A Check (✓) the embedded questions that have the same meanings as the direct questions.

1. What's wrong with Paul?

   ☑ Can you tell me what's wrong with Paul?

   ❏ Will Paul tell me what's wrong?

   ☑ I'm not sure what's wrong with Paul.

2. Will Beatriz call 911?

   ❏ I don't know if Beatriz will call 911.

   ❏ Should I call 911 if Beatriz doesn't?

   ❏ I wonder whether Beatriz will call 911.

3. Does Mariam know how to perform CPR?

   ❏ I don't know how Mariam is going to perform CPR.

   ❏ Could you tell me if Mariam knows how to perform CPR?

   ❏ Mariam doesn't know how to perform CPR.

B Unscramble the sentences. Write the words in the correct order.

1. how Tao / today / is feeling / know / do you

   _____

2. this week / to the doctor / Alicia will go / I'm sure

   _____

3. Anh / why / I / is in shock / wonder

   _____

4. you / tell / me / could / needs insulin / Mr. Duval / if

   _____

5. I / giving the medicine correctly / don't know / if / you are

   _____

C Change each direct question to an embedded question. More than one answer is possible.

1. Who is Don's doctor?

   <u>Can you tell me who Don's doctor is?</u>

2. What kind of surgery is Mrs. Popova having?

   _____

3. Where is the first aid class?

   _____

4. Why is Yuan calling 911?

   _____

D Complete the conversation between two co-workers. Use embedded questions.

Min-ji: Hi, Joe. (1) <u>Could you tell me where Kate is</u>?

Joe: Kate? Oh, she's at home. She's sick.

Min-ji: What's wrong with her?

Joe: (2) _____. I think
she might have the flu. But I think she's going to be out sick all week.

Min-ji: Hmm. (3) _____? I want to call her.

Joe: Sure. Her phone number is 555-2931.

Min-ji: Thanks, Joe. Hey, how late is FlowerMart open?

Joe: (4) _____. Why?

Min-ji: I thought we could go there and get Kate some flowers.

Joe: That's a good idea.

READ

Read the article. Circle the diseases that are mentioned.

Prevention Matters

There are many ways that people can protect their health. Below are some common screenings, treatments, and immunizations that are important for people of many ages.

Women's Health Screenings

Breast cancer is the second most common cause of cancer death for women in the United States. Luckily, it can be treated when found early. The test for breast cancer is called a mammogram. The risk increases with age, so women over age forty need to get a yearly mammogram. Women who have breast cancer in the family (a mother, sister) are at risk, so they should start having mammograms after age thirty-five. All women also need to get yearly pap tests. These are tests for cervical cancer and vaginal cancer. Women of any age can get these cancers, so women twenty-one and over should get a pap test every year.

Flu Shots

The flu, or influenza, is a virus that spreads from one person to another. You can get the flu through contact with someone or by breathing it in the air. You can also get the flu if you touch an object that has the virus on it, such as a door handle. Symptoms of the flu are fever, sore throat, cough, headache, chills, and muscle aches. Influenza season is November to April, so flu shots are given at this time. People can get a free shot to protect them from the flu virus. Children and old people, especially, should get flu shots. When people are sick with a cold, however, they should not get a flu shot because it can make them sicker.

Smoking Cessation

Smoking can lead to many diseases, including heart disease, stroke, many types of cancer, and lung disease. It is important to quit smoking if you are a smoker. People who have a smoking-related illness may be able to get free help to quit if they have Medicaid or other insurance.

Hepatitis B

Hepatitis B is a serious disease that is common in cities such as New York City, Atlanta, Chicago, and some cities in California. Hepatitis B is spread through blood or fluids, so hospital workers should get shots for it. You can talk to your doctor about getting free shots.

Medicaid, a U.S. government health program, covers many of the screenings mentioned above. Early prevention is important because it can stop people from getting sick. This also saves individuals and the government money. People should contact their doctors to discuss any questions they have about preventive health treatments, costs, and available resources.

CHECK YOUR UNDERSTANDING

A Read the article again. Highlight signal words that show cause and effect.

Reading Skill:
Recognizing cause and effect

To understand explanations in texts, look for causes and effects. An effect is what happened. A cause is why it happened. Certain words signal causes and effects, including *so*, *because*, *because of*, *therefore*, *lead to, result,* and *as a result.*

B Read the statements based on the article. Write *T* (true) or *F* (false).

_____ 1. The most common cause of cancer deaths in women is breast cancer.

_____ 2. Older women are more likely to get breast cancer than younger women.

_____ 3. Young women cannot get cervical cancer.

_____ 4. You can get the flu by breathing it in the air.

_____ 5. People should get the flu shot only when they are feeling well.

_____ 6. Hospital workers are at risk for getting hepatitis B.

C Complete the statements. Circle the correct answers.

1. Most women should be tested for cervical cancer _____.
   a. starting at age forty
   b. starting at thirty-five
   c. starting at twenty-one

2. Women should get screened for breast cancer if they _____.
   a. are younger than thirty-five
   b. have a sister or mother with breast cancer
   c. have a sister-in-law with breast cancer

3. Smoking can cause _____.
   a. cervical cancer
   b. hepatitis B
   c. heart and lung diseases and cancer

4. Hospital workers are at risk for hepatitis B because _____.
   a. the virus is found in patients' blood
   b. the virus is found in the air
   c. the virus is found on doorknobs

A Read the essay. Underline the sentences that give background information.

One of the most serious health problems in the United States today is obesity. Many people are overweight because they have bad eating habits. For example, many Americans eat one-third of their meals at fast-food restaurants. Fast food has a lot of calories—but customers might not realize just how many. I think that all fast-food restaurants should have to print on their menus the calorie amounts of the food they serve. If restaurants print their calorie counts, people will make better decisions about their diets.

Nutritionists say that most people should get about 750 calories at each meal. The meals at fast-food chains usually have many more calories than this. For example, a typical meal at one fast-food chain has 1,385 calories. And a Burger King Triple Whopper with cheese has 1,230 calories.

I think that people would order less fattening foods if they knew the calorie count of what they were eating. A friend of mine used to get a blueberry muffin and a latté every morning before work. Then the restaurant printed the calorie counts of their food items. When she found out that her snack was 740 calories, she stopped buying it. In just two weeks, she has lost four pounds.

If fast-food restaurants had to print the calorie counts of their foods, people would probably eat less of the fattening foods. Then, maybe the restaurants would start offering more healthful foods. This would be good for the health of customers and for the United States as a whole.

B What is the main argument? Circle the correct answer.

a. People are obese because they eat at fast-food restaurants.

b. Fast-food restaurants should print the calorie content of their foods.

c. People should stop eating at fast-food restaurants.

A **Match the words with their definitions. Write the letters.**

__e__ 1. treatment

a. the regular beat that can be felt as your heart pumps blood around your body

____ 2. pulse

b. information about something or someone, which is either written on paper or stored on a computer

____ 3. records

c. something added to improve your diet, especially a vitamin

____ 4. supplement

d. a physical condition that shows when you may have a particular disease

____ 5. symptom

e. a method that is intended to cure an injury or sickness

B **Use the words in Exercise A to complete the sentences.**

1. My doctor recommended that I take a calcium _____supplement_____.

2. The best _____ I know of for a cold is to rest and drink fluids.

3. The nurse put her fingers on my wrist to check my _____.

4. I asked my doctor to send all my _____ to the hospital.

5. She only had one _____ of diabetes. She was always thirsty.

C **Study the word map. Then create a word map of your own for the word *injury*.**

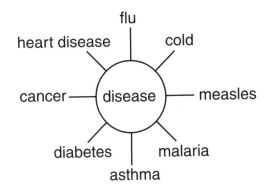

Learning Strategy:
Making word associations

When you learn a new word, what related words and ideas come to mind? Take a moment to think of and write down these associations. A word map is a good tool for making these associations. You can add these maps to your vocabulary cards and logs.

A Complete the sentences with the past perfect form of the verbs in parentheses.

Before the London Company founded the first permanent English colony in Jamestown,

John White ___*had established*___ a settlement on Roanoke Island in North Carolina. A man
             (**1. establish**)

named Sir Walter Raleigh _____ permission from Queen Elizabeth to explore
             (**2. receive**)

the area. After some men _____ a few trips to explore the island, about 100
             (**3. make**)

men, women, and children went to live there in 1587. John White led the group. The people

started to build a community. White's daughter, Virginia Dare, _____
             (**4. be**)

pregnant on the trip, and she gave birth to the first English child on the island.

White went back to England to get supplies. It was a very long and dangerous trip back to

England. Finally, when White arrived in

England, he got supplies to return to

Roanoke. However, he could not return

to Roanoke because Spain

_____ to attack
(**5. start**)

England. The British needed every ship

for this fight, so they took away his ship

and used it to fight the Spanish Armada.

Finally, White was able to return in 1590.

Queen Elizabeth sends Sir Walter Raleigh to America.

But by the time he arrived in Roanoke, the people _____. Today, it is still a
             (**6. disappear**)

mystery. No one is sure what happened to the people, and Roanoke is called The Lost Colony.

B Complete the conversation. Circle the correct word.

Anna: This summer, I saw a great play about early America.

Cesar: Really? I love American history. What was the play?

Anna: *The Lost Colony*. Did you know that some English people had (1.) ⟨already⟩ / **yet** tried
to establish a colony before Jamestown?

Cesar: No, I didn't. Tell me more.

Anna: The colony was called Roanoke. It was a small colony, and the people were in danger.
They needed help from England, so the leader, John White, left on a ship. But it took
him more than two years to come back. (2.) **By that time,** / **While** the people had
disappeared. The play was about what might have happened to them.

Cesar: Sounds interesting.

Anna: It was a great story, but the costumes were the best part. They were beautiful and
all new. I read about it in the program. There was a fire in the costume shop last year.
(3.) **By the time** / **Already** the fire was put out, many of the costumes had
(4.) **already** / **just** burned. The theater started raising money in September, and by
May, they had (5.) **already** / **just** gotten all the money for the new costumes.

C Complete the sentences. Use the past perfect.

1. Before George Washington commanded the Continental Army,

   _____*he had been a delegate to the First Continental Congress.*_____
   (he / be / a delegate to the First Continental Congress)

2. When Washington signed the Constitution,

   _____
   (no one else / sign / it / yet)

3. By the time Washington took office in 1798,

   _____
   (he / already sign / the U.S. Constitution)

4. Before he was president, _____
   (Washington / marry / Martha Custis)

5. Martha and George Washington lived in Philadelphia because

   _____
   (Washington, D.C. / not / become / the capital yet)

BEFORE YOU READ

Look at the words and definitions.

commit libel: to knowingly publish lies or something bad about someone with the plan to harm that person or to attack his or her character

forbidden: not allowed

obscenity: an offensive word, language, behavior, or action

prosecution: lawyers who try to prove in a court of law that someone is guilty of a crime

READ

Read the article. Name the amendment that guarantees U.S. citizens the freedom of speech.

The Freedom of Speech

Many people are surprised when they discover that U.S. citizens can openly disagree with the government and not be punished. This is because freedom of speech is protected by the First Amendment in the U.S. Bill of Rights. Citizens can express their thoughts without fear of prosecution by the government. The First Amendment protects the freedom of speech, but can U.S. citizens say *anything* they want? Not entirely. There are few exceptions.

Inappropriate Time, Place, or Manner

Expressing yourself at certain times and places may not be protected by the First Amendment. For example, you have the right to march in a protest. However, you do not have the right to make a noisy protest at 4:00 A.M. in a residential neighborhood.

Libel

The First Amendment does not allow you to commit libel against other people. That is, the law in your state may forbid you to tell a lie in order to harm someone, such as causing a person to lose his or her job.

Obscenity

According to the Supreme Court, the First Amendment does not protect the right to use obscene language. But people all over the country disagree about what is considered obscene and what is acceptable, especially for what children may see or hear.

Speech That Incites Violence

Using speech to encourage others to harm people, or to plan to overthrow the government by force, is not protected by the First Amendment. The exact laws about this type of speech vary by state.

What kind of speech is protected and forbidden remains a controversial issue. The issue is becoming even more controversial with the use of the Internet. Now, people post content on the Internet that may include violence, sex, and obscene language. Children may log on and see this content. In the future, the courts will have to make more decisions regarding what content is protected and forbidden, in order to best protect the rights of all citizens.

CHECK YOUR UNDERSTANDING

A Read the statements. Write *T* (true) or *F* (false).

__T__ 1. U.S. citizens can disagree with the government and not go to jail.

_____ 2. The Fifth Amendment protects freedom of speech.

_____ 3. The First Amendment protects you if you publish lies about someone.

_____ 4. People disagree about what is considered obscene.

_____ 5. Laws about speech that incites violence are the same in every U.S. state.

_____ 6. Courts will continue to make laws about free speech in the future.

B Complete the T-chart. The first definition is provided for you. Look at the article and a dictionary for help.

Word or phrase	Definition
1. Controversial	1. Something that causes a lot of disagreement between people because many people have strong opinions about it
2. Inappropriate Time, Place, or Manner	2.

Reading Skill:
Using a T-chart to take notes

Taking notes while you read will help you remember information. A T-chart is a simple tool that can help you organize your notes. T-charts have two columns and are very useful when you want to remember information connected with a list of dates or when you want to record definitions or examples.

DICTIONARY SKILL: Identifying stressed syllables

In English words of two or more syllables, at least one syllable has more stress, or force, than the other(s). Dictionaries use symbols to show which syllable receives the main, or primary, stress. Look at the entry and phonetic spelling from the *Longman Dictionary of American English (LDAE)* for the word *citizen*. Notice the symbol that this dictionary uses to show the main stress.

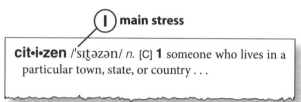

Many English words have more than one stressed syllable. Dictionaries use different marks to indicate which syllable receives the primary stress and which receives the secondary stress. Look at the word *citizenship*. Notice that the first syllable receives the main stress, and the fourth syllable receives the secondary stress. Different parts of speech within one word family often have different stresses.

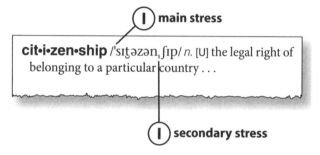

Look up the words in the chart. Circle the syllable that receives the main stress. If another syllable receives secondary stress, underline it.

Verb	Adverb	Noun	Adjective
automate	automatically	automation	automatic
colonize	X	colony	colonial
justify	X	justification	justified
represent	X	representation	representative
restrict	X	restriction	restrictive

WORD STUDY: Learning prefixes and suffixes

As you learned in Unit 1, a **prefix** is a word part added to the beginning of a word that changes the word's meaning. Like the prefix *dis-*, *un-* means "not" or "the opposite of."

A Look at the chart. Add the prefix *un-* to each base word to create a new word. Write the new word and its meaning in the chart.

Base word	Prefix	New word	Definition
1. able	un-	unable	not able
2. usual	un-	unusual	not usual or typical
3. common	un-		
4. just	un-		

You also learned in Unit 1 that a **suffix** is a letter or group of letters added to the end of a base word, which can change a word's part of speech and meaning.

The suffix *-ment* means "action, state, or place." The suffixes *-tion, -sion,* and *-ion* mean "the act, state, or result of." These suffixes can be added to verbs to create nouns.

B Look at the chart. Add the suffix *-ment* to each base word to create a new word. Write the new word and its meaning in the chart.

Base word	Suffix	New word	Definition
1. argue	-ment		
2. enforce	-ment		
3. govern	-ment		
4. harass	-ment		

READ

Read the article. What type of information is listed with bullets? Circle the best answer.

a. questions for a civics class

b. categories on the civics test

c. materials for the civics test

Reading Skill:
Using text structure and formatting

To better understand what you read, notice a text's structure and formatting. **Boldfaced type**, bullets (•), and color can help you find the main points. Bullets can also help you identify items in a series.

TEST TIME

American Government
- Principles of American Democracy
- System of Government
- Rights and Responsibilities

American History
- Colonial Period and Independence
- 1800s
- Recent American History and Other Important Historical Information

Integrated Civics
- Geography
- Symbols
- Holidays

There are many steps to becoming a U.S. citizen. If you meet the requirements and fill out the forms, you will have to pass a naturalization test with the U.S. Citizenship and Immigration Services (USCIS). In one part of this test, most people will be asked to read, write, and speak English. In the other part of the test, people are given an oral test to make sure they know about U.S. civics—history and government.

There are one hundred possible questions on the civics tests. Applicants will be asked ten of the one hundred questions. They must answer at least six correctly to pass this part of the test. The questions are divided into three categories and nine subcategories:

You can get a copy of all of the questions and answers on the USCIS website. It lists all one hundred questions and gives answers in note form.

There are many things you can do to prepare and study for the test. The USCIS provides many materials you can buy online, such as books, flash cards, and even a pocket-sized Declaration of Independence and U.S. Constitution. You can also make your own materials from the free questions and answers you can get online. It's a good idea to study with someone and practice since the test is oral.

Here are examples of questions from the test and their answers:

American Government		
Principles of American Democracy What is the supreme law of the land? *The Constitution*	**System of Government** Who makes the federal laws? *Congress*	**Rights and Responsibilities** How old do citizens have to be to vote for President? *18*
American History		
Colonial Period and Independence Who wrote the Declaration of Independence? *Thomas Jefferson*	**1800s** What territory did the United States buy from France in 1803? *The Louisiana Territory*	**Recent American History** Who did the United States fight against in World War II? *Japan, Germany, and Italy*

Source: www.uscis.gov

CHECK YOUR UNDERSTANDING

A **Read the article again. Then read the statements. Write *T* (true) or *F* (false).**

_____ 1. The naturalization test includes an English test and a civics test.

_____ 2. You need to get 100 questions right to pass the test.

_____ 3. The three major categories on the civics test are American Government, American History, and Integrated Civics.

_____ 4. The USCIS gives only the test questions online, not the answers.

B **Take the civics test. Answer the questions about civics. Look at the article to check your answers.**

1. What is the supreme law of the land called in the United States?

_____

2. Who wrote the Declaration of Independence?

_____

3. How old do citizens have to be to vote for President?

_____

4. Who did the United States fight against in World War II?

_____

LIFE SKILLS

Look at the map that shows battles from the U.S. War of Independence. Write _T_ (true) or _F_ (false).

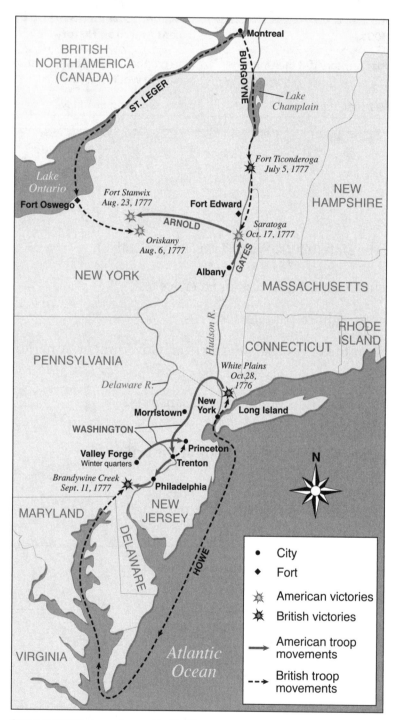

Source: © 2009 Cartography provided by Maps.com

_____ 1. New Hampshire borders Lake Ontario.

_____ 2. Morristown is west of New York City.

_____ 3. Long Island is west of Connecticut.

_____ 4. Trenton is located on the Delaware River.

STUDY SKILL: Interpret a historical map

Look at the map again. Circle the correct answer to each question.

1. Which battle was fought in Pennsylvania on September 11, 1777?

   a. Brandywine Creek

   b. Valley Forge

   c. Morristown

2. How did General Howe travel from New York to New Jersey?

   a. on foot only

   b. by boat and on foot

   c. on horseback and on foot

3. When was the Battle of Fort Ticonderoga fought?

   a. August 25, 1777

   b. August 6, 1777

   c. July 5, 1777

4. What body of water did General Burgoyne travel on?

   a. the Chesapeake Bay

   b. Lake Ontario

   c. Lake Champlain

5. Valley Forge was the winter headquarters of which general?

   a. Howe

   b. Washington

   c. Arnold

6. When was the Battle of White Plains?

   a. August 27, 1776

   b. October 28, 1776

   c. December 26, 1776

7. Which rivers did Washington's army cross?

   a. the Delaware and the Hudson

   b. the St. Lawrence and the Delaware

   c. the Hudson and the Mohawk

A Read the e-mail to the mayor. Find and correct seven errors.

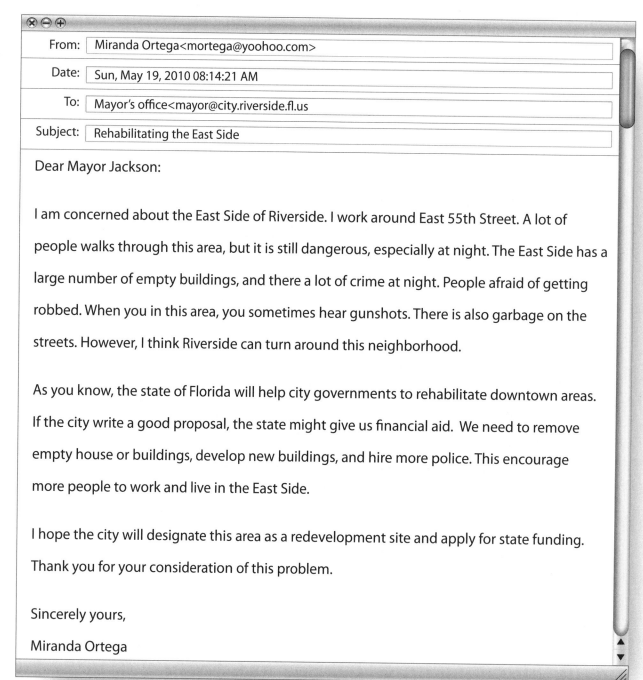

From: Miranda Ortega<mortega@yoohoo.com>

Date: Sun, May 19, 2010 08:14:21 AM

To: Mayor's office<mayor@city.riverside.fl.us

Subject: Rehabilitating the East Side

Dear Mayor Jackson:

I am concerned about the East Side of Riverside. I work around East 55th Street. A lot of people walks through this area, but it is still dangerous, especially at night. The East Side has a large number of empty buildings, and there a lot of crime at night. People afraid of getting robbed. When you in this area, you sometimes hear gunshots. There is also garbage on the streets. However, I think Riverside can turn around this neighborhood.

As you know, the state of Florida will help city governments to rehabilitate downtown areas. If the city write a good proposal, the state might give us financial aid. We need to remove empty house or buildings, develop new buildings, and hire more police. This encourage more people to work and live in the East Side.

I hope the city will designate this area as a redevelopment site and apply for state funding. Thank you for your consideration of this problem.

Sincerely yours,

Miranda Ortega

B What problems does this e-mail discuss? What solutions does it give? Write in your notebook.

A Match the words with their definitions. Write the letters.

_____ 1. automatically

a. to start something such as a company, system, or situation, especially one that will exist for a long time

_____ 2. colony

b. a set of ideas about what is right and wrong

_____ 3. federal

c. without thinking about what you are doing

_____ 4. establish

d. the right to be given attention first, before other people and things

_____ 5. principles

e. relating to the central government of a country that consists of several states

_____ 6. priority

f. a group of people who have left their home country to live in a new place

B Complete the sentences with the words from Exercise A.

1. The ____federal____ government is the government of the whole country.

2. Jamestown was the first permanent English _____ in North America.

3. By 1750, the English decided to _____ thirteen colonies.

4. When any child is born in the United States, that child is _____

   considered a U.S. citizen.

5. The _____ of the U.S. Constitution are life, liberty, and the pursuit of

   happiness.

6. When citizens petition the government to bring family members to the United States, they

   receive _____ over non-citizens.

A Complete the sentences with the clauses below. Write the clauses.

1. If you are arrested for drunk driving, _____.

2. If you do not have money for an attorney, _____.

3. If the police want to question you, _____.

4. If you answer questions from the police, _____.

5. If you do not have an attorney with you, _____.

   a. they will first inform you of your legal rights

   b. your answers might be used against you in a court of law

   c. remember that you have the right to remain silent

   d. you will need to take a blood alcohol test

   e. the state will provide you with one

B Unscramble the sentences. Write the words in the correct order.

1. the state will appoint one for you / if / the court believes you do not have enough money for an attorney

   _____

2. his or her fingerprints will be checked / if / someone / commits a criminal offense

   _____

3. have a good lawyer / he or she can help you / if you / to tell your side of the story

   _____

4. you have been arrested / if / will be able to make / you / one phone call

   _____

C Rewrite the sentences with the *if* clause at the beginning.

1. Joseph might get a fine if he jaywalks.

   _____

2. Mr. Ramos might call the police if Robert and Jay trespass.

   _____

3. Carolina's mother might pay her legal expenses if Carolina can't afford an attorney.

   _____

4. You can call an attorney if you are arrested.

   _____

5. The boys will be arrested if Mr. and Mrs. Novak call the police.

   _____

D Write future real conditional sentences with the words in parentheses. Start the sentences with *if*.

1. he / commit / a crime / he might get arrested

   _____

2. you / need / to hire / an attorney / it could be expensive

   _____

3. he / trespass / someone might call the police

   _____

4. the police / stop / her / for drunk driving / she will have to take a breath alcohol test

   _____

5. she / get / a DUI on her driving record / her insurance might go up

   _____

E MAKE IT PERSONAL. Write about the law in your native country. If you get arrested for drunk driving, what happens? If you can't afford a lawyer, what happens? Write in your notebook.

READ

Read the article. What does *suffrage* mean?

The Struggle for Suffrage

Women won the right to vote in 1920, but this right did not come easily. It took over fifty years. First, only men with property had the right to vote. After the Civil War, in 1870 the right was extended to African-American men, but women were still excluded from voting. Nevertheless, they did not give up. The National American Woman Suffrage Organization (NAWSA) fought for women's right to vote, state by state, but failed.

Then in 1913, the struggle for suffrage grew more intense. NAWSA organized a parade in Washington, D.C. The parade was set for the day before the new president, Woodrow Wilson, was to be sworn in. This would attract publicity because the press (reporters) was focused on Washington. The result was spectacular. Over 5,000 people marched on Washington for women's voting rights. The parade was dramatic. Some women and children were dressed in beautiful costumes as Freedom, Justice, and Peace. One reporter said, "It was one of the most . . . beautiful spectacles ever staged." At first there was no violence. The women marched down the street. Then crowds of men stopped them and yelled at them, tripping them and shoving them. The police did little to help. One hundred marchers were hurt and were taken to the hospital.

The protest succeeded in getting national attention for the suffrage movement. People had different reactions. NAWSA said the protest was amazing. But a government official said, "Nothing like this [injured women] would happen if you would stay at home."

Overall, many Americans were sympathetic to the women.

In 1916, the National Women's Party was begun to fight for women's voting rights. This new organization wanted to pass an amendment to the U.S. Constitution. To publicize their cause, women tried something never done before. They picketed outside the White House. The picketing started in 1917 and lasted many months, leading to the arrest and imprisonment of many women. Finally, in the summer of 1920, the Nineteenth Amendment was passed, giving women the right to vote. The struggle had been won at last.

CHECK YOUR UNDERSTANDING

A **Read the article again. Write *T* (true) or *F* (false).**

_____ 1. For a long time, only men with property had the right to vote in the United States.

_____ 2. Women were given the right to vote soon after the Civil War.

_____ 3. The Fifteenth Amendment gave women the right to vote.

_____ 4. To win the right to vote, women held protests and got publicity from newspapers.

_____ 5. The Nineteenth Amendment gave women the right to vote.

B **Read the statements and write *F* (fact) or *O* (opinion).**

_____ 1. Some women and children were dressed in costumes as Freedom and Justice.

_____ 2. "The parade was one of the most beautiful ever staged."

_____ 3. Over 5,000 people marched on Washington.

_____ 4. "Nothing like this would happen if you would stay at home."

> **Reading Skill:**
> Distinguishing fact from opinion
>
> When you read a text, notice which statements are facts and which are opinions. A fact is a piece of information that you can prove with evidence. For example, a fact can be checked by looking at a reliable source, such as an encyclopedia or a history book. An opinion is a belief or feeling. Opinions often begin with the words *I think, I believe, I feel, probably, perhaps,* or *maybe.* They may express a judgment about whether something is good or bad, safe or dangerous, fair or unfair.

C **Look at the article. Write the dates.**

_1920_ 1. Women were granted the right to vote.

_____ 2. The right to vote was given to African-American men.

_____ 3. A suffrage parade was organized in Washington, D.C.

_____ 4. The National Women's Party was founded.

_____ 5. The National Women's Party began picketing the White House.

D **MAKE IT PERSONAL. What are the voting rights in your native country? Does everyone have the right to vote? Write in your notebook.**

LIFE SKILLS

Bullying is common in the workplace. Look at the chart and answer the questions about the study.

1. In the study, what is the most common type of mistreatment of workers?

   verbal abuse

2. If an employer gives a worker a job that is unsafe, what is this called?

   _____

3. If an employee deserves to be promoted but is denied a promotion, what is this called?

   _____

4. If an employer gives an employee an impossible task, what is this called?

   _____

5. If an employer is cruel or offensive to employees, what is this called?

   _____

Most common mistreatment at work

Verbal abuse (shouting, swearing, sarcasm, threats to safety, name calling)

53.3%

Improper behaviors/actions (threatening, intimidating, cruel, hostile, offensive)

52.5%

Abuse of authority (undeserved evaluations, denial of advancement, unsafe assignments, etc.)

46.9%

Interference with work performance (making it impossible for target to succeed at job)

45.4%

Destruction of workplace relationships

30.2%

Source: © 2007 Workplace Bullying Institute

STUDY SKILL: Interpret charts

A Look at the chart. It shows the percentages of men and women who bullied or who were targets of bullies. Read the statements about the study. Write *T* (true) or *F* (false).

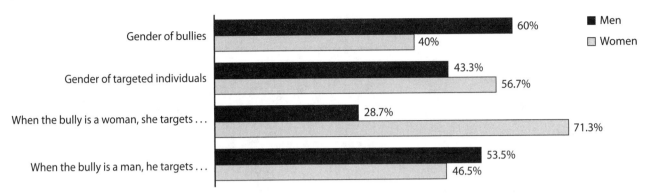

Source: © 2007 Workplace Bullying Institute

_____ 1. More women were bullies than men.

_____ 2. More women were targets of bullying than men.

_____ 3. When the bully was a man, the bully targeted men more than women.

_____ 4. According to the study, women who bully in the workplace usually bully other women.

B Look at the pie chart. It shows actions that employers took when bullying was reported. Read the statements about the study. Write *T* (true) or *F* (false).

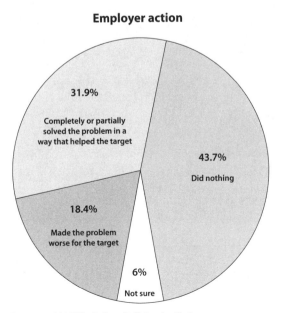

Source: © 2007 Workplace Bullying Institute

_____ 1. More than half of employers did not stop the bullying.

_____ 2. More than half of employers solved the problem.

_____ 3. 18.4 percent of employers made the situation worse.

READ

Read the article.

LOOK AND LISTEN

When driving, you will often encounter flashing lights or special situations that require you to yield to traffic. Make sure you understand and obey traffic laws.

Picture this: You are driving on the road. You look in the rearview mirror and you see flashing red lights. You hear a siren. What do you do? Don't panic—pull over. When driving, you must pull over for police cars, fire engines, and ambulances if they have sirens or flashing lights turned on. Move your car to the right edge of the road. If you have committed a traffic violation, the police will pull off the road behind you. For fire engines and ambulances, pull over on the side of the road until the vehicle passes you. Then you may pull back onto the road. If you are in an intersection when you hear a siren or see lights, make sure you are safely through the intersection before pulling over.

Usually you must stop for a red or yellow traffic signal, but in some situations you must follow the directions of traffic police instead. For example, when traffic lights are not working, traffic police direct traffic. If the traffic light is green but an officer motions you to stop, you need to stop. Or if the light is red, the traffic officer might motion you to go. Do as the officer says and drive through the light, but do so carefully and cautiously.

When you encounter a school bus, pay special attention. You must pull over when you see a stopped school bus with its red lights flashing. You must do this no matter what side of the road the bus is on. In other words, pull over even if it is going in the opposite direction. This is to protect children who are getting on or off the bus. There may be children crossing the road. Once the red lights stop flashing, you may get back on the road. However, be sure to look carefully for children before you pull back onto the road.

The next time you hear a siren or see flashing lights, remember to stay calm, and stay out of trouble by getting off the road!

CHECK YOUR UNDERSTANDING

A **Read the article again. Write *T* (true) or *F* (false).**

_____ 1. You should stop your car in the middle of the road when you hear a siren.

_____ 2. You should pull over if you hear a siren.

_____ 3. You should pull over for all police cars—those both with and without flashing lights.

_____ 4. If you are in the middle of an intersection and you hear a siren or see lights, you need to drive through the intersection and then pull over over afterward.

_____ 5. Sometimes traffic police must direct the traffic instead of traffic lights.

_____ 6. You need to pull over if you see a school bus with red lights flashing.

_____ 7. When traffic police are working, you must follow their directions, not the streetlights.

B **Match each statement with an inference that can be made. Write the letter.**

_____ 1. When driving, you must pull over for police, fire engines, and ambulances if they have sirens on.

_____ 2. When you encounter a school bus, pay special attention.

_____ 3. Drive through the light, but do so carefully and cautiously.

> **Reading Skill:**
> Making inferences
>
> When you make an inference, you make a logical guess about something that is not directly stated in the text, based on other information that is provided. In other words, you "fill in" information.

a. A police officer might tell you to drive through a red light, but you still need to be careful not to hit cars and pedestrians.

b. Children can get off a bus suddenly, so you need to be careful.

c. It is illegal to keep driving when you see flashing lights from an emergency vehicle behind you.

DICTIONARY SKILL: Formal vs. informal language

A dictionary entry for a word will often tell its *usage*, or how that word is commonly used. Some words are only used in informal contexts. Other words are commonly used in writing, but not in speech. Look, for example, at these two dictionary entries for words that have a similar meaning but are different in tone.

> **law·less** /ˈlɔlɪs/ *adj.* (formal) not obeying the law, or not controlled by law

> **crooked** /ˈkrʊkɪd/ *adj.* **1** not straight: *crooked teeth* **2** (informal) not honest: *a crooked cop*

The labels a dictionary uses—such as *formal*, *informal*, *spoken*, *written*, *law*, or *technical*—are usually explained in the first few pages of the dictionary.

Read each pair of sentences. Which words are formal, and which are informal? Write *F* (formal) or *I* (informal).

1. I'm going to call the <u>cops</u>. __I__

   We notified the <u>police</u>. ____

2. The criminal was <u>apprehended</u> at the scene of the crime. ____

   They <u>arrested</u> the guy right away. ____

3. He <u>went on and on asking questions</u> for ages. ____

   They <u>interrogated</u> the suspect for an extremely long time. ____

4. The criminal was <u>incarcerated</u> for twelve years. ____

   He was <u>put in the slammer</u> overnight. ____

5. Jaywalking is <u>a minor violation</u> in our town. ____

   Jaywalking? That's really <u>no big deal</u>. ____

WORD STUDY: Understanding word families

In Unit 4, you learned that most English words belong to a "family" of words that have similar meanings. For example, the verb *rob* means "to steal something"; *robbery*, a noun, means "the act of stealing something."

A Complete the chart with the correct forms of the words. More than one form may be possible for some parts of speech. Use your dictionary to look up the forms and to learn their meanings.

Verb	Noun	Adjective
amend	amendment	
	guidance	guided
	murder	
	rejection	
		suspended

B Complete each sentence. Use the correct part of speech of the word in parentheses. Use the word families chart above as a guide.

1. The Senate voted in favor of the ___amendment___ (amend).

2. We didn't know why the judge decided to _____ (rejection) the lawyer's

   request.

3. My counselor gave me some very good _____ (guide) about being on a jury.

4. The jury was told to _____ (suspension) all judgment until all the evidence

   had been presented.

5. The act of _____ (murderous) is a serious crime.

6. We were very disappointed by the city council's _____ (reject) of the proposal

   for a new recreation center.

A **Read the essay. There are six errors. The first one is corrected for you. Find and correct five more.**

Traffic Fines Are Everywhere!

OK, so you know how to drive in Los Angeles. If you go over the speed limit in L.A., you will get a ticket. If you run a red light, you'll get a ticket. And if you ~~will not~~ *don't* stop at a stop sign and a police officer sees you, guess what you will gets? That's right: a ticket!

It's not all that different in Mexico City. In both cities, drivers who get moving violations—in other words, drivers who break a traffic law when the car is moving—will have to pay a fine. But that's not all. In addition to a fine, the driver receives a penalty point for every moving violation.

So, what does that mean? It means that if you will get a ticket for a moving violation, you not only will have to pay a fine, you'll get a point. In California, if you have four points, you will lose your driver's license. In Mexico City, if you accumulate twelve points, you will had lose your license.

In Mexico City, if you will talk on a hand-held cell phone while driving, you will get one point. In California, you will be fined $20 for the first offense—but you will not receive a point. In Mexico City, if you will be driving in a bus lane, you will receive six penalty points. In L.A., you will get only one point.

So, drivers need to be aware of the traffic laws as well as the fines and penalties, no matter what country they are in. It pays to drive safely, no matter where you are.

B **Read the questions. Circle the best answers.**

1. How are L.A. and Mexico City similar?
   a. They both have bad traffic.
   b. Both give fines and penalties to drivers who violate traffic laws.

2. How are L.A. and Mexico City different?
   a. There are different penalties for cell phone use, moving violations, and driving in bus lanes.
   b. Hand-held cell phones are legal in Mexico City.

A Match the words with their definitions. Write the letters.

_____ 1. former

_____ 2. impose

_____ 3. material

_____ 4. penalty

_____ 5. regulation

_____ 6. suspect

a. a thing or object

b. a punishment for not obeying a law or rule

c. an official rule or order

d. happening or existing before, but not now

e. someone who may be guilty of a crime

f. to force something, such as a rule, on someone

> **Reading Skill:**
> Grouping words with the same root
>
> As you already know, many English words come from or contain Greek or Latin roots. Once you know the meaning of a root, you can recognize it in new words and, often, figure out the meanings of those words.

B Study the word map for the Latin root *spec.*

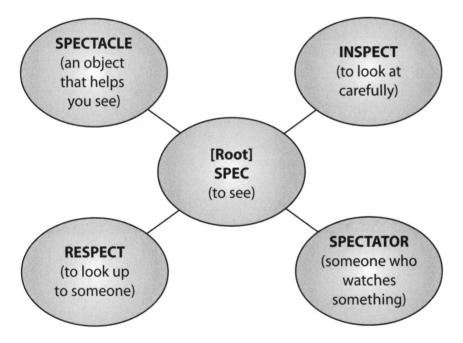

C In your notebook, create a word map for the roots *port* or *dic.* Use a dictionary to look up the meanings of the words with that root. Write the root in the center of the map. Place words that contain the root in the surrounding circles. Include definitions.

Unit 9: Saving the Planet

Lessons 1 & 2: Life Skills and Study Skills

LIFE SKILLS

Look at the recycling calendar and guidelines. Write *T* (true) or *F* (false).

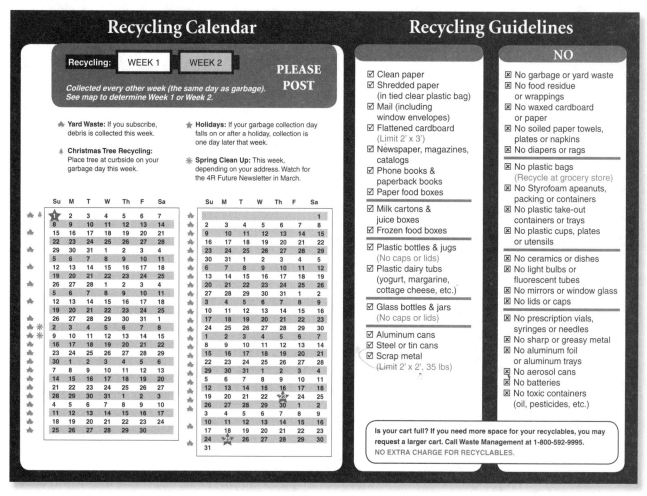

Source: © 2006 City of Auburn, Washington

_F_ 1. You may recycle plastic bottles with the bottle caps.

_T_ 2. You may not recycle waxed cardboard.

_F_ 3. You may recycle glass jars and mirrors.

_F_ 4. You can recycle aerosol cans and aluminum cans.

_F_ 5. The size limit for recycling cardboard is 2″ by 3″.

STUDY SKILL: Read a recycling brochure

Circle the correct answer to each question.

Collection Time

SET OUT

♦ Please put all containers out before 6:00 a.m. within five feet of the street without blocking sidewalks, driveways or parking. Please remove them from the curb as soon as possible after collection.

♦ Limit 32-gallon container weight to 65 lbs., and please do not put yard debris, liquids or hazardous waste in the garbage or recycling, for your Collector's safety. Thank you.

MISSED COLLECTION

♦ Please call 1-800-592-9995 for missed collections. Leave the container(s) out until the end of the next business day.

WEATHER DELAYS

♦ If weather conditions prevent safe collection, a double load of garbage and recycling will be collected at no extra charge on your next collection day.

Yard Debris

YARD DEBRIS is collected from gray carts provided to residences that subscribe for yard debris service.

♦ Yard debris is organic material from your yard, including leaves, grass and branches under 3 inches in diameter by 3 feet long. Shredded paper may also be "mixed in" with yard waste. *No sod, dirt, rocks, concrete or lumber.*

♦ Extra yard debris may be put in your own containers (32-gallon, 65-lb. limit), heavy paper bags or bundles (4' x 2' limit). Label them "yard debris" and put them next to the gray yard debris cart at least three feet from your garbage. *No plastic bags, please.* There is an **additional charge for each extra unit of yard debris.**

♦ Yard debris is collected weekly April through November, and every other week December through March (see calendar). Please call 253-931-3038 for new service set-up.

1. By what time do people have to put out their garbage?

   a. 5:00 A.M.   b. 6:00 A.M.   c. 7:00 A.M.

2. Where must people put their garbage cans?

   a. in a driveway   b. on the sidewalk   c. within 5 feet of the street

3. What is the weight limit for a 32-gallon garbage can?

   a. 32 lbs.   b. 96 lbs.   c. 65 lbs.

4. What should people do if they miss a collection?

   a. call 1-800-592-9995   b. call the mayor   c. leave containers out for one week

5. Which of these is yard debris?

   a. dirt   b. leaves   c. rocks

READ

Read the article. Who is the blogger? Circle the correct answer.

a. **Darlene**

d. **Dan**

b. **Jin-Su67**

e. **Tania4Earth**

c. **Stephensschein**

Reading Skill:
Understanding the style and structure of blogs (web-logs)

Blogs are like journals or diaries; they usually contain personal reactions or comments. Most blogs are written in an informal, conversational style and are organized in reverse chronological order (from last to first), that is, the most recent item is posted first. Many blogs have a comments section where readers can submit their reactions to the "blogger," or writer.

Dan's Recycling and Greening Blog

November 6 |recycling|
Great news, readers! New York City mayor Michael Bloomberg signed a law that requires large stores to offer a plastic bag recycling program and to sell reusable bags. He is following what many countries in Europe are doing to reduce the number of plastic bags being used. Last month, I bought several bags at my local grocery store for $1 each and I bring them with me every time I shop. It's a very easy way to help the environment. If I forget my bags and have to take plastic ones, I recycle them at home. I use them for small amounts of trash instead of buying large trash bags.

Darlene says …
This is good news, Dan. Maybe there will be less litter now. I always see lots of plastic bags blowing around in the city. Maybe this will reduce the amount of garbage on the street.

November 4 |recycling|
Hello, my recycling friends! Did you know that many office stores will recycle batteries? The other day, I took several batteries and an old ink cartridge to an office store in my neighborhood. They gave me a $3-off coupon for my next purchase! It's another great way to help the environment and to save money.

November 1 |recycling|
Recycle and reuse! I'm having a secondhand sale in my apartment building. I encourage all of you to get involved and plan a similar event in your building or neighborhood. People can save money by buying used items, and others can get rid of items they don't use anymore.

Jin-Su67 says . . .
I planned something similar. I organized a community drive. All of the donated items were given to a local charity.

October 28, 2008 |technology|
Hi readers. If you want to save some energy with your PC, there are a number of very simple tips you can use.

* Unplug the computer when it's not in use. The computer actually uses energy when it's in "off" state, just like a TV "standby" state.
* Enable the sleep function on your hard drive and monitor. This is an option in most operating systems, including Windows and Mac OS X.

Stephensschein says . . .
You're right, Dan. I always unplug my computer. Don't forget to tell readers about cell phone chargers, too. When you aren't charging your cell phone, make sure to unplug the charger. If you don't, the charger uses energy. Devices like that are called vampires.

Tania4Earth says . . .
Is it the same with my coffeemaker? The light that shows the time is always on. Should I pull out the plug when I'm not using it?

Stephensschein says . . .
That's right, Tania. Coffeemakers that have lighted clocks use energy when they are plugged in even if they are turned off. They don't use that much energy, but it's better to unplug them. You'll save money on your utility bill if devices like that are turned off.

CHECK YOUR UNDERSTANDING

Read the blog again. Read the statements. Write *T* (true) or *F* (false).

_F_ 1. Europe is watching the U.S. example and recycling plastic bags like the United States does.

_T_ 2. Mayor Michael Bloomberg has passed a recycling law for New York City.

_F_ 3. All office supply stores recycle batteries.

_F_ 4. Computers do not use energy when they are turned off but still plugged in.

_T_ 5. You should unplug coffeemakers when not in use.

_T_ 6. Devices like cell phone chargers can waste electricity if you do not unplug them.

_F_ 7. Only Dan can answer questions that people post on his blog.

DICTIONARY SKILL: Understanding grammar codes

Many dictionaries provide helpful information about grammar and usage within word entries. For example, they use codes to let you know whether a noun is countable or uncountable. You can use the grammar information in a dictionary to improve your grammar and usage. Read the Grammar Codes from the *Longman Dictionary of American English (LDAE)*.

[C] countable; shows that a noun can be counted and has a plural form: *We planted an orange* **tree**. | *Children love to climb* **trees**.

[U] uncountable; shows that a noun cannot be counted and has no plural form: *I need some* **peace** *and quiet.* | *a glass of* **milk**.

[I] intransitive; shows that a verb has no direct object: *I'm sure I can* **cope**. | *Our food supplies soon* **ran out**.

[T] transitive; shows that a verb is followed by a direct object which can be either a noun phrase or a clause: *I* **like** *swimming, playing tennis, and things like that.* | *I* **hope** *I'm not disturbing you.* | *We never* **found out** *her real name.*

[I, T] intransitive or transitive; shows that a verb may be used with or without a direct object: *Bernice was* **knitting** *as she watched TV.* | *She was* **knitting** *a sweater.*

Use the grammar codes above and the dictionary entries below to answer the questions.

plan·et /ˈplænɪt/ *n.* [C] **1** PHYSICS a very large round object in space, that moves around a star, such as the Sun: *Mercury is the smallest planet*

pol·lute /pəˈlut/ *v.* [I,T] to make air, water, soil, etc. dangerously dirty: *Toxic waste is* **polluting** *the air/ocean/environment.* —**polluter** *n.* [C]

1. Is *planet* a countable or an uncountable noun?

   _____

2. Can *pollute* be used as a transitive verb, an intransitive verb, or both?

   _____

WORD STUDY: Understanding collocations

Some words are often paired with each other. We call these word pairs **collocations**. There are many collocations about the environment, like the words *water pollution* and *air pollution*.

A Look at the chart below. Write the word that often comes before the words in each list. Use the words in the box.

> environmental   global   ~~greenhouse~~   public   solar

1. *greenhouse*	2. _____	3. _____	4. _____	5. _____
effect	interest	energy	disaster	economy
gas	transportation	system	impact	warming

B Complete the sentences with the words in the box.

> environmental   ~~global~~   greenhouse   public   solar

1. Many scientists think that _____*global*_____ warming is melting the ice at the North and South Poles.

2. We hope to be able to use _____ energy to heat our new house.

3. _____ gases increase the temperature of the Earth.

4. If nuclear waste is not disposed of properly, it results in a(n) _____ disaster.

5. The city is urging people to take _____ transportation rather than driving their cars.

A Use the information below to write sentences using a form of the verb *wish*.

Who	What	Should have
Silvia	organized the event in a week	taken a month to plan it
Ermias	brought in his cans and paper	brought in his glass bottles, too
Nicole	stayed home	come to the event
Rafal	recycled his old cell phone	given his cell phone to his brother
Rose	threw away the cups after lunch	recycled the cups

1. *Silvia wishes that she had taken a month to plan the event.*

2. _____

3. _____

4. _____

5. _____

B Complete the paragraph with the correct forms of the verbs in parentheses.

   Plastic bags cause pollution. As a result, many countries are now banning plastic bags. In 2002, Ireland taxed plastic bags. Before 2002, shoppers used around 1.2 billion plastic bags each year. If Ireland _____ (1. not / tax) plastic bags, plastic bag use would have remained high. Bangladesh also banned plastic bags after many floods in the capital city blocked sewage lines. If Bangladesh _____ (2. ban) plastic bags earlier, the bags might not have blocked drains. If they _____ (3. not / block) the drains, the capital city might not have flooded. South Africa has also banned plastic shopping bags. If South Africa _____ (4. not / ban) the plastic bags, the problem would have continued. Finally, Zanzibar outlawed plastic bags because they made the island ugly. The island survives on tourism, so it needs to be clean. If it _____ (5. not / got rid of) plastic bags, tourism might have been hurt.

C Write sentences with past unreal conditionals. Use pronouns when needed.

1. Rita

If clause: her co-workers / own / cars

Result clause: she / carpool

<u>If Rita's co-workers had owned cars, she would have carpooled.</u>

<u>Rita would have carpooled if her co-workers had owned cars.</u>

2. Mrs. Shi

If clause: she / know about the coupon

Result clause: she / recycle her batteries

_____

_____

3. Omar and Irma

If clause: Yolanda / tell them about the recycling center

Result clause: they / take their bottles to the recycling center

_____

_____

4. Mindy

If clause: her clothes / fit her cousin

Result clause: she / give her clothes to her cousin

_____

_____

5. Zhu

If clause: he / be / aware / of the price of gas

Result clause: he / not / drive so much

_____

_____

READ

Read the article. What does the photo show? Circle the correct answer.

a. a new kind of architecture

b. a roof with environmental benefits

c. a sun roof

> **Reading Skill:**
> Using visuals
>
> Using visuals—such as photographs and drawings—will help you better understand what you read. Notice what the visual shows. Read any labels or captions carefully. Sometimes a visual will give information that is not in the text.

GREEN WORK

Majora Carter is an environmental activist from the Bronx in New York City. She started Sustainable South Bronx in 2001. The organization's mission is to "address land use, energy, transportation, water and waste policy, and education to advance the environmental and economic rebirth of the South Bronx, and inspire solutions in areas like it across the nation and around the world."

One of the organization's projects is the South Bronx Greenway Project. The plan is to make a bike and walking path by the waterfront. This will provide clean, green spaces for Bronx residents and others to get exercise. Carter is hoping to have the city change trucking routes so that the outdoor pathway will be less polluted.

Sustainable South Bronx also works with the community to create green roofs. Green roofs are roofs that contain a layer of soil and plants.

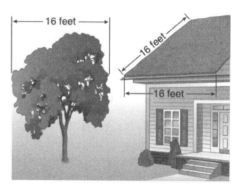

A 16-square-foot patch of a green roof produces the same amount of oxygen as a tree that is 16 feet in diameter. The roof takes much less time to grow and costs much less money to plant.

Green roofs reduce the amount of rainwater that runs into the streets and the sewage system. The roofs absorb the rain before it is polluted, and it is released slowly back into the air. The green roofs also produce oxygen, which is helpful to the environment. Green roofs cost twice as much as traditional roofs, but they have some benefits. They reduce the cost needed to cool a building because they provide extra insulation. Green roofs also provide temporary jobs, as people are needed to design, waterproof, and install the roofs. Small crops can also be grown on the roofs.

Sustainable South Bronx also offers free training programs for the workers. For instance, they have programs in hazardous waste cleanup, tree pruning, OSHA training, and herbicide application.

What Carter started in 2001 has now grown to an organization with a staff of about twenty people, all helping to green the South Bronx.

A green roof reduces heating and cooling costs.

CHECK YOUR UNDERSTANDING

A **What is the purpose of the diagram and caption? Circle the correct answer.**

a. to show that a tree and a patch of roof produce the same amount of oxygen

b. to show someone how to install a green roof

c. to show how trees are used to make green roofs

B **Read the statements. Write *T* (true) or *F* (false).**

_T_ 1. Majora Carter works for an environmental organization.

_F_ 2. Sustainable South Bronx wants to make a bike and walking path.

_F_ 3. New York City has agreed to change trucking routes for the walking path.

_T_ 4. Sustainable South Bronx creates green roofs.

_T_ 5. Green roofs are covered with soil and plants.

_F_ 6. Green roofs are inexpensive to build.

C **Complete each sentence. Circle the correct answer.**

1. Sustainable South Bronx's goals include _____.

   a. changing the way land is used in the Bronx

   b. reducing rainwater

   c. making green spaces for Brooklyn residents

2. Green roofs produce _____.

   a. carbon dioxide

   b. oxygen

   c. recycled plant materials

3. When rain falls on green roofs, the water _____.

   a. does not go back into the air

   b. goes back into the air

   c. runs off the building and falls into the street

A Read the personal narrative. There are nine errors. The first one is corrected for you. Find and correct eight more.

>   *had*
> I own an old SUV. I have it for a long time now—my brother gave it to me, used, six years ago. If
>
> I had realize how bad the gas mileage was, I might had told my brother to give the car to
>
> someone else. Back then, though, gas was cheaper than it is now. Also, people didn't worry about
>
> the environment like they do now. SUVs are bad for the environment.
>
>   Some people I know told me that I should trade in my SUV for something smaller and more
>
> economical. The problem is, I need a big car. I have four kids between the ages of three and
>
> eleven, and I drive my husband and my uncle to work every morning. When I go to the grocery
>
> store, the shopping bags fill up most of the car. Also, I feel safe in my SUV.
>
>   About a month ago, I start looking at used cars online. Then I went to a car lot. The salesman
>
> suggest a sedan. He said sedans has much better gas mileage, and they easier to park. But I still
>
> prefer a larger car.
>
>   Last Friday I found a great car—a hybrid SUV, a 2006 Saturn. It gets 24 miles to the gallon,
>
> and it still has a lot of room. It's expensive, though, for a used car—$13,000! After I saw the ad, I
>
> look up the trade-in value of my SUV. My car is only worth $7,000! I wish I have traded it in
>
> three years ago, when it was worth $14,000!
>
>   So I'm going to buy the car. I'm glad I will save on gas mileage.
>
> **Magali Brito**

B Look back at the personal narrative. Underline the words and phrases that show time order.

Review and Expand: Vocabulary

A Match the words with their definitions.

<u>d</u> 1. civic leader

      2. generation

      3. impact

      4. natural resources

      5. reconstruct

      6. traditional

a. all the people in a society or family who are about the same age

b. all the land, minerals, energy, and other assets that exist in a country

c. to build again

d. an authority working for the local government

e. following ideas or ways that have existed for a long time

f. the effect or result of an event or situation

> **Learning Strategy:**
> Getting to know a word's history
>
> The history of a word is called its etymology. Most big dictionaries include etymologies. Learning a word's origin and original meaning can help you remember the word and how to use it. Look back at the dictionary entries for the words *environment* and *planet* on page 110. Study the history of each word at the end of the definition, after the word *origin*. Why do you think that *planet* comes from a word that means "wanderer"?

B Use a dictionary to look up the origins of the following words. Then create a vocabulary card for each word. Include the word's etymology on the card.

1. etymology _____

2. cosmos _____

3. geology _____

LIFE SKILLS

**Look at the diagram that shows how to install video cable to an LCD TV.
Answer the questions.**

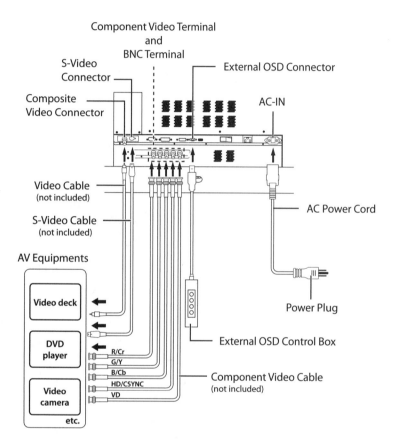

1. What are three kinds of AV equipment?

   _____

   _____

   _____

2. How many connectors are included? _____

3. How many cables can you connect to the AV equipment? _____

4. How many power outlets do you need to plug the power plug into? _____

STUDY SKILL: Read a manual

**Read the following part of the LCD TV manual and the statements below.
Write *T* (true) or *F* (false).**

Placement precautions

- Avoid placing the unit in humid or dusty places or where it can be exposed to excessive heat.
- Do not step on or set anything on the AC power cord. DAMAGE TO THE AC POWER CORD IS A SAFETY RISK AND CAN CAUSE A FIRE.
- Do not connect the unit to the same AC outlet with appliances with motors such as refrigerators.
- Keep the unit away from water. If water gets inside the unit, unplug the AC power cord immediately. Do not plug in the unit again.
- Never cover the rear ventilators with cloth.

Handling precautions

- WARNING: The AC power cord and cables on this product contain chemicals, including lead, known to the State of California to cause cancer and birth defects. *Wash hands after handling.*
- Never insert or remove the power cord with wet hands.
- Do not remove any parts that are held in place with screws. (The unit does not contain any user-serviceable items.)
- Maintain standard room temperature (5°C to 35°C, or 41°F to 95°F) during use.

_____ 1. You should not connect the LCD unit to an AC outlet if the outlet is also connected to a refrigerator.

_____ 2. If water spills on the unit, wipe it carefully with a towel. Do not unplug the AC unit.

_____ 3. If you think part of the unit is broken, you can open the unit with a screwdriver and replace the parts yourself.

_____ 4. Do not expose the unit to very hot or very cold temperatures.

_____ 5. If the AC power cord gets damaged, it could start a fire.

DICTIONARY SKILL: Using example sentences

Dictionaries usually give examples that show how a word is used in the context of a sentence. If a word has several different meanings, often an example phrase or sentence is given for each meaning. Reading these sentences can help you understand the different meanings and uses of a word. Study the example phrases and sentences in these dictionary entries.

---

da•ta /'deɪt̬ə, 'dæt̬ə/ *n.* [U, plural] **1** information or facts: *He's **collecting data** for his report.* | *The team gathered **data on** voting patterns in each state.* **2** IT information stored and used on a computer: *This laptop can **store** as much **data** as many larger PCs.*

---

in•ter•net /'ɪnt̬ɚˌnɛt/ *n.* **the Internet** IT a system of connected computers that allows computer users around the world to exchange information syn **the Net, the Web**: *I found information about the college on the Internet.*

---

net•work¹ /'nɛt̚wɚk/ *n.* [C] **1** a group of radio or television stations that broadcast many of the same programs in different parts of the country: *the four biggest TV networks* **2** IT a set of computers that are connected to each other so that they can share information: *network administrators* | *I wasn't able to log onto the network.* | *Three-quarters of the traffic on their network consisted of e-mails.* **3** a system of lines, tubes, wires, roads, etc. that cross each other and are connected to each other: *the freeway network* | *the network of blood vessels in the body* | *The GPS system is base on a network of 24 satellites sending out radio signals.* **4** a group of people, organizations, etc. that are connected or that work together: *Trina had developed a good **network of** business contacts.*

network² *v.* **1** [I] to meet other people who do the same type of work, in order to share information, help each other, etc.: *Conferences can be a great opportunity to network.* **2** [T] IT to connect several computers together so that they can share information: *This system allows you to network all your computers.*

Four of the sentences below have errors. Use the information in the dictionary entries above to correct them. The first one is done for you.

1. She collected ~~datas~~ data from many different places.

2. Manuel and Kim worked as networks administrators for a large company.

3. Check the reviews of that computer on the Internet before you buy it.

4. Our computers were not working because network was down.

5. Her brother spends two hours a day surfing the Internets.

WORD STUDY: Abbreviations

Some words in English are really abbreviations, or short forms, of longer words or phrases. For example, *deli* is an abbreviation for *delicatessen*.

There are two other types of abbreviations that are often used in terms that have to do with technology: acronyms and initialisms. Initialisms use the first (or initial) letter of each word. The letters are pronounced separately: *U.S., FBI, CIA, PC, CD, FYI*. Acronyms also use the first letter of each word—but the letters are pronounced as one new word: NATO and AIDS.

Look up the abbreviations in a dictionary. Write the full forms in the chart below. Indicate whether the abbreviation is an acronym (A) or an initialism (I).

Word	Full form	Initialism (I) or acronym (A)?
1. PC	personal computer	I
2. LAN		
3. CD		
4. DVD		
5. PIN		
6. VR		
7. PR		
8. NASA		
9. ASAP		
10. HTML		

READ

Read the article. What is the author's purpose?

Reading Skill:
Identifying an author's perspective

Authors write for different reasons. They write to inform, to entertain, or to persuade. Sometimes, an author has more than one purpose for writing. To figure out why an author wrote a text, ask yourself: Is the text giving me information about a subject? Is it trying to persuade me to agree with the author's opinion?

Try a Virtual or Video Tour

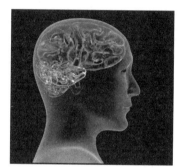

A virtual tour of the human brain

Can you imagine visiting a place without actually going there? Virtual and video tours make this possible. A virtual tour is a simulation of a real location made with photographs. The shots of still (unmoving) photographs in a virtual tour make you feel like you are in a place. A video tour is a motion video of a location. Unlike a virtual tour's static wrap-around feel, a video tour feels as if you are walking through a location. Virtual and video tours have many purposes.

First, virtual tours can help you make a decision about something before you buy it. For example, you can look at pages of a book online to see illustrations and even read sample pages. When you look at a book online, it is always a virtual tour because you see one image at a time. If you are buying a house, you can look on real estate websites and often take a virtual tour of the house. This allows you to see the exterior and interior rooms of the house. Then you might know if you are interested in seeing the house up close.

Virtual tours are also very helpful for planning a trip. You can take a virtual tour of a hotel before you make a reservation. You can also look for a virtual or video tour of the place you want to visit online. For example, you could see videos of places to see and things to do in Hawaii. This can help you plan your trip and decide what you want to see before you get there.

Virtual and video tours are also helpful in gaining information. For example, you can take virtual tours of some museums that allow you to read and see information, and it seems like you are there, instead of looking at your computer screen. You can also take many virtual tours of government sites to learn more about the government. Some of the tours are also on video. For example, if you visit http://www.whitehouse.gov/history/life/video/index.html, you can get a video walking tour of several famous rooms in the White House.

Virtual tours will also be important for the future of medicine. Physicians will use virtual and video tours to learn more about complex parts of the body or to do surgery. This technology is already being used today.

Whether you are making a purchase, traveling, or learning new information, virtual and video tours give a glimpse of places or things that you could never see otherwise.

CHECK YOUR UNDERSTANDING

A Read the statements. Write *T* (true) or *F* (false).

_____ 1. Virtual tours are taken with a series of photographs.

_____ 2. Video tours are made with unmoving, still photographs.

_____ 3. Virtual and video tours are helpful for making decisions such as purchases.

_____ 4. If you buy a book online, you can sometimes view pages of the book.

_____ 5. It is possible to look inside the human body by using computer technology.

B Complete the statements. Circle all the answers that are true.

1. If you are buying a house, you can sometimes see _____.

   a. a virtual tour with photographs

   b. a video tour of the rooms inside the house

   c. a video tour of the neighborhood where you want to buy the house

2. If you are planning a trip, a virtual tour is good for _____.

   a. finding out information about the place you are visiting

   b. seeing your hotel

   c. making your airline reservations

3. The U.S. government _____.

   a. does not have virtual tours but is planning them for the future

   b. offers virtual tours of all government buildings

   c. offers virtual tours of some of its institutions like the White House

4. Virtual tours _____.

   a. will help us to better understand the human body

   b. are not yet being used by doctors

   c. are part of our medical insurance system

C MAKE IT PERSONAL. What kind of virtual or video tours would you like to take? What would you like to see or find out about? Write in your notebook.

A Unscramble the sentences. Write the words in the correct order.

***The Matrix*, with Keanu Reaves**

1. is an environment / that is produced by a computer / virtual reality

   _____

   _____

2. is an idea / that is very popular in films / virtual reality

   _____

3. that is about virtual reality / is a famous film / *The Matrix*

   _____

4. is a technology / that / by health professionals / virtual reality / is also used

   _____

5. shows ways / that a surgeon / should cut / virtual reality / during surgery

   _____

B Underline the correct answers. Sometimes both answers are possible.

Lilia: Hi, Brad. What are you doing?

Brad: I'm taking a cooking class (1.) **that** / **who** has an online teacher. Look!

Lilia: Wow. Is that the woman (2.) **who** / **that** has a TV show?

Brad: Yes. It's Chef Zhang from the show *Zhang's Way*. It's the show (3.) **which** / **that** teaches you to make different foods in five easy steps. It's a video (4.) **who** / **that** has clips from her TV show.

Lilia: What's that? Is that a link (5.) **who** / **that** takes you to the recipe?

Brad: Yes, it is. And this is the link (6.) **who** / **which** takes you to a video of another chef. See? This is Chef Jones. He's the man (7.) **who** / **which** makes the same recipes as Chef Zhang, but with healthier ingredients.

C Rewrite the sentences with *who* or *which*.

1. SkyTech is a game that uses simulation to teach basic airplane maneuvers.

   SkyTech is the game which uses simulation to teach basic airplane maneuvers.

2. Mr. Bui is the coach that uses virtual reality to help his students learn how to pitch a baseball.

   _____

3. *Biology of a Horse* is an exhibit that can be toured online.

   _____

4. *VisitMe* tours are tours that are becoming more popular than traveling.

   _____

5. Computer programmers that work with simulators usually get paid a lot.

   _____

6. Athletes that use virtual reality programs often improve their game.

   _____

D MAKE IT PERSONAL. Complete the sentences with *who*, *which*, *that*, and your own ideas.

1. Virtual tours are tours _____.

2. Virtual reality seems real to the person _____.

3. Video tours are tours _____.

4. I like movies _____.

BEFORE YOU READ

Read the definitions.

> *Download*: to transfer a file from the Internet to your own computer
> *Moderate*: to judge something
> *Upload*: to transfer a file from your computer to the Internet

READ

Read the article. What is YouTube? What are three of its problems?

Almost everyone who goes online has heard of YouTube, LLC. This video-sharing website has millions of users. Currently, about 100 million videos are viewed every day on YouTube.

How YouTube Works

YouTube users can upload, view, and share video clips. Users upload everything from TV clips, movie clips, and music videos to their own amateur short original videos. Unregistered users can watch the videos. People who want to upload their own videos need to register first with YouTube.

YouTube's Rules

YouTube's terms of service have rules it demands users to follow:
- no video uploads that contain defamation
- no commercial advertisements
- no copyright violations
- no videos that encourage criminal behavior
- Videos that show or suggest sex can be watched only by registered users age eighteen or older

YouTube's Problems

Since YouTube was started in 2005, it has had difficulty enforcing rules. About 65,000 videos are uploaded every day on YouTube. The company moderates the uploads and removes videos that are against the rules. But because there are so many videos, sometimes inappropriate or unlawful videos get through.

—Copyright violation. Many users have illegally uploaded movies. In March 2007, Viacom sued YouTube for $1 billion for copyright violation. Viacom said that YouTube illegally showed MTV videos and other shows owned by Viacom.

—Deciding what is "defamation" or "offensive." YouTube removes from its website videos that contain defamation or are offensive. However, people have different opinions about what defamation is and what is offensive.

—Age restriction. YouTube has no way to stop a child under eighteen from registering on YouTube and watching offensive content.

➡ Next

Blocking of YouTube
Several countries have blocked access to YouTube since its beginning, including China, Iran, Morocco, and Thailand. Countries have blocked YouTube because some videos were against their religious or cultural beliefs. On February 23, 2008, Pakistan blocked YouTube for three days because some content was considered offensive toward Islam. YouTube has also been blocked by some countries like China when videos criticized the governments of those countries.

Revenue
A final problem YouTube has had is making money for its owner company, Google™. Although millions of people view its website every month, YouTube has trouble getting advertisers to post ads. Why? Many sponsors are afraid of advertising with the company because of its copyright problems and because of videos on the website that may be offensive.

← Back

CHECK YOUR UNDERSTANDING

A **Read the article again. Write *T* (true) or *F* (false) for each statement.**

_____ 1. YouTube does not allow people to put commercials on its website.

_____ 2. YouTube allows videos that show how to make bombs.

_____ 3. Viacom has sued YouTube for stealing its property.

_____ 4. Pakistan blocked YouTube for political reasons.

_____ 5. YouTube makes a lot of money for Google™.

B **Complete the timeline with facts from the article.**

Some Events in YouTube's History

1. _____ 2. _____ 3. _____

2005 — Mar 2007 — Feb 2008

> **Reading Skill:**
> Using a timeline
>
> When you are reading about a historical event, it is often useful to organize your notes onto a timeline. Timelines are usually divided into specific time periods, such as decades (ten-year periods) or centuries. Events from long ago are placed on the left; more recent events go on the right. Use your timelines to review what you have read.

C MAKE IT PERSONAL. **Have you ever visited YouTube? If you visit it in the future, what would you like to look up on it? (music videos, dance, etc.) Write in your notebook.**

Read the autobiographical essay. There are seven errors. The first one is corrected for you. Find and correct six more.

I grew up in a poor section of São Paulo City, Brazil, that ~~was~~ called Cidade Tiradentes. Ten years ago, most people did not have access to computers and the Internet—it was much too expensive. Then, in 2003, the local government opened up a free Internet café. My life changed.

I spent an hour a day, that is the maximum time allowed a person on the café computer. I wanted to learn computer skills who would help me find a good job. The telecenter also offered courses to people which had never used computers. I took courses in word processing, the Internet, and spreadsheet software.

Six months later, I got a job as an administrative assistant to Sr. Suarez. Sr. Suarez, that was the vice president of a large bank. A year later, there was an opening in another office of the bank in Los Angeles. I applied for the position—and got it!

I was going to move to a new city, in a new country—and I had to find an apartment. Thankfully, I knew how to use the Internet. I went online and found a great website described all the different neighborhoods in Los Angeles. Then I searched the Internet for rentals in the neighborhood and found a great place.

I've been living and working in Los Angeles for two years now. I've learned how to use all kinds of software, and now I'm going to college at night. I think that the telecenter in Cidade Tiradentes gave me an advantage in life helped me learn, grow, and move to new places.

A Match the words with their definitions. Write the letters.

_____ 1. criteria

_____ 2. data

_____ 3. engineer

_____ 4. innovation

a. the introduction of new ideas, methods, or inventions

b. someone who designs or builds machines

c. facts or standards used in order to help you judge or decide something

d. information or facts

B Complete the sentences with the words from Exercise A.

1. He took many courses in order to become a computer _____.

2. They collected _____ on the number of students who shop online.

3. The team received an award for its _____ in the field of wireless communications.

4. The teacher explained the _____ she would use to judge our work.

> **Learning Strategy:**
> Learning "new" words
>
> Language is always changing. New words are created, and existing words are used in new ways. In the past twenty years, many new words related to technology have become a part of the English language. Words such as *e-mail, texting, blog,* and *cyberspace* are very common—and can be found in most large dictionaries.

C Create a section in your vocabulary log for the following categories. Add new words to the log as you hear or read them. Some common examples are provided for you.

Computers	Internet	Personal communication
bug	browser	blogging
click	website	e-mail
spreadsheet	World Wide Web	texting
virus	Google™	

Answer Key

TO THE STUDENT

Page v, Exercise A

Lesson 1: life skills and study skills
Lesson 2: grammar
Lessons 3 & 4: reading
Lesson 5: grammar
Lesson 6: reading
Expansion: dictionary skills and word study
Lessons 7, 8, & 9: writing
Review & Expand: vocabulary

Page v, Exercise B

1. page 6, page 10
2. page 3
3. page 14
4. page 15

Page v, Exercise C

Dictionary Skill: Understanding a dictionary entry
Word Study: Learning prefixes and suffixes

Page v, Exercise D

1. the answer key
2. There are different correct answers.

UNIT 1

Page 2, Life Skills

A. Store manager
B. Security guard
C. PT installation technician trainee
D. Medical office assistant

Page 3, Study Skill

1. computer software engineers
2. 12.6
3. 2,114
4. 35.4 percent or 148,000
5. registered nurses, computer software engineers, accountants and auditors, and computer systems analysts

Page 4, Exercise A

1. Joy wants to work with children in a school.
2. Min Hee enjoys helping patients in a hospital setting.
3. Dan needs to make a lot of money to support his family.
4. Eduardo does not want to work on a computer all day.
5. Jun does not mind taking risks.
6. Luis would like to learn to cook at a culinary school.
7. Maria Amelia prefers to work with co-workers./Maria Amelia prefers working with co-workers.
8. Feng plans to follow instructions carefully at her new job.
9. Jean Paul hopes to become an engineer.
10. Alexandra does not like to have so many rules and regulations at work./Alexandra does not like having so many rules and regulations at work.

Page 5, Exercise B

Joy:	to find out
Mrs. Ito:	working
Joy:	love
Mrs. Ito:	being
Joy:	want
Mrs. Ito:	studying
Joy:	to pay, don't like
Mrs. Ito:	working, talking
Joy:	would like
Mrs. Ito:	to take
Joy:	to take

Page 4, Exercise C

Answers will vary.

Page 6, Read

Highlighted answers will vary and may include:

construction
restoring old buildings
restoration
teacher
history teacher
math and science teachers
finance
banking
financial analysts

Page 7, Exercise A

1. T
2. F: William Keenoy specializes in restoration.
3. F: In 2002, William Keenoy recognized that there would be less work in new construction.
4. T
5. F: In the future, there will be a high demand for math and science teachers.
6. T
7. T

Page 7, Exercise B

1. b, d   2. c   3. a, e

Page 8, Exercise A

1. b   2. a   3. b   4. a   5. c

Page 8, Exercise B

1. working   4. applying
2. starting   5. reaching
3. painting

Page 9, Exercise C

1. of going
2. at listening
3. for helping
4. by finishing
5. on going
6. in taking
7. about studying

Page 9, Exercise D

I work at a hospital and many of the patients speak Spanish. I am good at **learning** new languages. I speak Italian and English, so I think it will be easy to learn Spanish. I'm thinking about **taking** a class at a community center in my neighborhood. I'm also interested **in finding** a person to practice with. Maybe I can help that person by **practicing** English. I plan on **getting** as much exposure to Spanish as I can. Eventually, I'll try reading Spanish magazines.

Page 9, Exercise E
Answers will vary.

Page 10, Before You Read
b

Page 11, Exercise A
1. b   2. a

Page 11, Exercise B
1. b   2. a   3. b   4. b

Page 11, Exercise C
Check (✓) the following:
change the deadline; find a way to
get a skill you need to reach the goal;
change the way you reach the goal

Page 12, Exercise B
1. example sentence
2. part of speech
3. syllabification, stress mark,
   pronunciation/phonetic spelling
4. syllabification
5. stress mark

Page 13, Exercise A
3. discontinue: not continue
4. disagree: not agree

Page 13, Exercise B
Answers may vary. Possible answers
include:

3. exchangeable: able to be exchanged
4. acceptable: good enough for a
   particular purpose

Page 13, Exercise C
Answers may vary. Possible answers
include:

1. distrust: not trust
2. disobey: not obey
3. affordable: not expensive

Page 14, Exercise A
1. I am very calm and a good
   problem solver.
2. I have good communication skills.

Page 14, Exercise B
Supporting details for topic sentence (1):
I can deal with stress well and make
   fast decisions.
I also have good judgment in a crisis.

Supporting details for topic sentence (2):
I speak English and Spanish, so I can
   communicate with doctors and
   patients who might not speak each
   other's languages.

Page 15, Exercise A
1. d   2. c   3. b   4. e   5. a

UNIT 2
Page 17, Exercise A
1. b   3. b   5. a
2. a   4. b   6. b

Page 17, Exercise B
Answers may vary. Possible answers
include:

1. schools, hospitals, libraries,
   senior care facilities, city run
   organizations, and not-for-profit
   organizations, like food pantries.
2. Marianne volunteered because she
   grew up in a neighborhood with
   gangs and wanted to give hope to
   young people who were trying to
   leave gangs.

Page 17, Exercise C
Answers will vary.

Page 18, Exercise A
1. Desired **Occupation**: Chef
2. **Experience**:
3. Prepared meals for **breakfasts**,
   lunches, and dinners
4. Made Chinese dishes and **seafood**
5. Helped with ordering and
   receiving of supplies
6. Developed new dinner and lunch
   menus for the **restaurant**

Page 18, Exercise B
- No, the jobs under **Experience** are
  listed in the wrong order. The most
  recent position should be listed
  first.
- The e-mail address is missing.

Page 19, Study Skill
1. 595
2. 962
3. professional degree
4. 3.0
5. professional
6. 3.8

Page 20, Read
Eva had better references.

Page 21, Exercise A
1. F   3. T   5. F
2. T   4. F   6. T

Page 21, Exercise B
1. c   2. a   3. d   4. b

Page 21, Exercise C

	Reference
0	Your current employer.
2	A co-worker who is now a manager at your old company.
1	An employer you worked for three years ago.
2	An employer you worked for part-time two years ago.
0	A close friend of the family.

Page 22, Exercise A
1. has not found
2. has worked
3. has prepared
4. has written
5. has cooked
6. has completed
7. has passed
8. has received

Page 22, Exercise B

1. Mark has written a résumé.
2. Mark hasn't sent copies of his résumé to employers.
3. Mark has researched jobs online.
4. Mark has looked for volunteer work.
5. Mark hasn't started volunteer work.

Page 23, Exercise C

1. has lived, for four days
2. has been, for two days
3. has known, for one day
4. has volunteered, for three days

Page 23, Exercise D

1. Hilda has worked in hospitals since she was a teenager.
2. Dadi has had his computer since 2006.
3. Carla has lived here since 1997.
4. Mr. and Mrs. Pham have known Veronica since September.
5. Manuel has been an HVAC technician since the fall.

Page 24, Exercise A

1. jazz
2. jeans
3. jet set
4. jigsaw puzzle
5. John Doe
6. journalist
7. judo
8. justice
9. justice of the peace

Page 24, Exercise B

howl, hubcap, human

Page 25, Word Study

Part of Speech	Meaning
1. noun	1. accident
2. verb	2. suddenly stop working
3. noun	3. opinion or feeling you have about someone
4. noun	4. mark left by pressing something into a soft surface
5. verb	5. provide people with something they want or need
6. noun	6. an amount of something that is available
7. noun	7. effect that an event or situation has on someone or something
8. verb	8. have an important or noticeable effect on someone or something

Page 26, Exercise A

1. Jim has been working at a bank since 1992.
2. Hassan and Penelope have been studying English for three years.
3. Te-Chao hasn't been studying English for long.
4. Victoria and Kyle have been using the Internet all day.
5. I've been writing my résumé.

Page 26, Exercise B

1. I've been looking for work since November.
2. Ben has learned new computer skills.
3. Kamila has been studying Spanish since 2007.
4. Jenni has taken an Excel 1 computer class.
5. Ms. Rios and Mr. Lee have just finished interviewing four people for the job.
6. Roberto has practiced for his job interview.

Page 27, Exercise C

Dress for Success® is a company that gives professional clothes to women who do not have enough money to buy them. Where does Dress for Success® get its clothing? Both volunteers and even clothing companies **have given** suits to the organization in the past. The company **has helped** over 450,000 women so far. Dress for Success® **has also started** a career center. Since it started, women **have learned** (or **have been learning**) computer skills to help them search for jobs.

Nancy Lubin started the company in 1996 in the United States. Since then, it **has expanded** to four other countries. Joi Gordon **has been working** as the executive director of Dress for Success® Worldwide since 2002. She now has a staff of over 50,000 people. In addition, many volunteers **have worked** (or **have been working**) at Dress for Success® over the years.

Page 27, Exercise D

Answers will vary.

Page 28, Writing

line cook; five years relevant experience; cost analysis; budgeting and purchasing; plan menus and invent new dishes; safety certified

Page 29, Exercise A

1. f
2. a
3. b
4. e
5. c
6. d

Page 29, Exercise B

1. employment agency
2. ambitious
3. human resources (HR) department
4. retail

Page 29, Exercise C

sales: customer, retail
employment: employment agency, human resources (HR) department

UNIT 3

Page 30, Dictionary Skill

1. driver
2. distracted
3. identify
4. phrasal verb
5. somebody/ someone

Page 31, Word Study

1. steering wheel
2. headlight
3. windshield wiper
4. rearview mirror
5. cell phone
6. emergency brake
7. gas pedal
8. gear shift
9. highway patrol
10. traffic jam/traffic light

Page 33, Check Your Understanding

Answers may vary. Possible answers include:

1. You can call roadside assistance.
2. You should practice so that you know you can do it correctly before it happens.
3. You need to keep a spare tire, wrench, screwdriver, carjack, and reflecting triangles in your car.
4. Children should be outside of the vehicle and out of the way of traffic.
5. Tighten the lug nuts with the wrench once your vehicle is on the ground.
6. You should check to make sure that everything is correct and tight.

Page 34, Exercise A

1. run into
2. breaks down
3. jack up
4. figure out
5. pull over
6. flag down

Page 34, Exercise B

1. into
2. down
3. out
4. on
5. in
6. over
7. up

Page 35, Exercise C

1. Make sure you fill it up.
2. There's no room for passengers, so you need to clean it out.
3. It's starting to rain, so turn them on.
4. Ivan picked her up and they went for a drive.
5. When we stopped at a rest stop, I let him out of the car.
6. Have you figured them out yet, or are we still lost?

Page 35, Exercise D

1. I have to pick my brother up at 3:00.
2. Julie turns her lights on when she drives at night.
3. Did Guy think the problem over carefully?
4. (inseparable phrasal verb, cannot be rewritten)
5. (inseparable phrasal verb, cannot be rewritten)

Page 35, Exercise E

Answers will vary.

Page 36, Life Skills

1. $286.00
2. $210.00
3. $303.00
4. $378.00
5. $350.00
6. $280.00

Page 37, Exercise A

USA Casualty Insurance Company

Page 37, Exercise B

1. Tatiana Rostov
2. inside the insured vehicle
3. Dodge
4. 12/05/2010–12/05/2011
5. 1-555-530-8222

Page 39, Exercise A

1. The signal turned red.
2. Maria answered a call on her cell phone.
3. The signal turned green.
4. The car behind Maria accelerated.
5. The car behind Maria hit her.

Page 39, Exercise B

1. Ivan was driving behind a car.
2. Ivan pulled into the left-hand lane to pass the car in front.
3. Ivan lit a cigarette.
4. Ivan pulled into the right-hand lane.
5. Ivan smashed into the other car.

Page 39, Exercise C

1. Dipak left the airport to take a customer home.
2. Dipak looked down at a map.
3. Dipak noticed a motorcycle in front of his car.
4. Dipak slammed on the brakes and turned the wheel.
5. Dipak drove off the city street.
6. Dipak drove over a curb and hit a fire hydrant.

Page 39, Exercise D

Answers will vary.

Page 40, Life Skills

1. I-495
2. south, right
3. left
4. slowly
5. east, the cemetery
6. left, north

Page 41, Study Skill

1. c
2. a
3. g
4. e
5. d
6. h
7. b
8. f

Page 42, Exercise A

Topic sentences:

People should not use cell phones while driving.

There is a lot of evidence that using a cell phone while driving is reckless and dangerous.

Cell phones, both hand-held and hands-free, are equally dangerous.

Driving requires responsible behavior.

Unrelated details:

Of course, drinking while driving is not a very good idea, either.

The drivers in the study—two of them were women—were from Fresno, California.

Sometimes I think people should not be allowed to listen to the radio or talk while driving, either.

Page 42, Exercise B

1. People should not use cell phones while driving.
2. (A study found that) just listening to a phone conversation consumes 37 percent of a person's attention span.
3. Hands-free phones are equally as dangerous as hand-held phones.

Page 43, Exercise A

1. d   3. a   5. b
2. c   4. f   6. e

Page 43, Exercise B

1. interior   3. professional
2. equipment   4. distracted

Page 43, Exercise C

1. workers
2. tools
3. roads for fast traffic
4. official documents about my car

UNIT 4

Page 45, Exercise A

2
1

Page 45, Exercise B

1. F   4. T   7. T   10. F
2. F   5. F   8. T
3. T   6. F   9. F

Page 45, Exercise C

1. When you first see lightning, count to 30. If you hear thunder before you reach 30, go indoors for at least 30 minutes.
2. Pipes can conduct electricity if lightning hits your home.

Page 46, Exercise A

1. The accident might have hurt the workers.
2. The hurricane could have destroyed many houses.
3. The fire chief should have evacuated the building.

4. The police should have warned the town.
5. The building manager should have collected the trash cans.

Page 46, Exercise B

1. have evacuated, have stayed home
2. have watched the news, have gone to work
3. have locked her doors, have been robbed
4. have prepared an emergency kit for their home, have had to sit in the dark for five hours

Page 47, Exercise C

Jesse: might not have
Linh: should have been
Jesse: should have, might not have, could have been
Linh: should have been

Page 47, Exercise D

Answers will vary.

Page 48, Dictionary Skill

1. safe   3. disaster
2. uproot   4. flood

Page 49, Exercise A

Verb	Noun	Adjective
center	center	central
confide	confidence	confident
damage	damage	damaged damaging
discriminate	discrimination	discriminating
prevent	prevention	
X	safe safety	safe
survive	survival survivor	surviving
trap	trap	X

Page 49, Exercise B

1. central
2. confidential
3. damage
4. discrimination
5. prevention
6. survive
7. trapped

Page 50, Exercise A

1. reflectors   3. helmet
2. hand brakes   4. sewer grate

Page 50, Exercise B

Answers will vary.

Bicycle accidents can be avoided if certain rules are followed.

Page 51, Exercise C

1. T   3. T   5. F
2. F   4. F   6. F

Page 51, Study Skill

1. 52 percent   3. a
2. 7 percent

Page 52, Read

Answers will vary. Possible answers include:

employees trip over objects; slipping on wet floors; sprain or strain muscles; shocks; hearing loss; cancer (lung cancer); viral infection (rubella, tuberculosis)

Page 53, Exercise A

1. Slips and Trips
2. Carcinogens
3. Hearing Loss
4. Shocks
5. Other Biohazards
6. Sprains and Strains

Page 53, Exercise B

1. T   3. T   5. F
2. T   4. F

Page 53, Exercise C

1. b   2. d   3. a   4. c

Page 54, Life Skills

1. a   2. a   3. b   4. c

Page 55, Study Skill

1. chemical hazard
2. excessive noise

3. extreme temperatures
4. worker motion or position
5. electrical hazard

Page 56, Read

Imperatives: Follow these safety tips; identify the most common sources; do not leave the room; turn off the stove; make sure that all flammable materials are kept away; turn it off immediately; do not place electrical cords; cover all unused outlets; never place candles; blow out all candles; do not use candles; install alarm systems; make sure every floor; test the alarms; consider installing a home sprinkler; have an escape plan; try to have two escape routes; practice your escape plans

Signal words: First; After; Finally

Page 57, Exercise A

1. b 2. d 3. e 4. a 5. c

Page 57, Exercise B

1. comply   4. substance
2. toxic   5. sturdy
3. furnish

Page 57, Exercise C

Answers will vary.

UNIT 5

Page 58, Read

b

Page 59, Exercise A

1. Do   4. Don't   7. Do
2. Don't   5. Don't
3. Do   6. Do

Page 59, Exercise B

1. Do It   3. Do It
2. Ask for It   4. Say It

Page 60, Read

c

Page 61, Exercise A

1. D   3. D   5. A   7. B
2. A   4. B   6. D

Page 61, Exercise B

1. b   2. a   3. b

Page 61, Exercise C

1. D   2. T   3. F   4. F   5. F

Page 62, Exercise A

1. (No) Michael can't speak Spanish, although he can speak Portuguese.
2. ✓
3. ✓
4. (No) Hai did very well at the interview although he didn't make eye contact.
5. (No) Susan won't go to the interview on Tuesday unless she gets a babysitter.

Page 63, Exercise B

1. unless   4. unless
2. Although   5. Unless
3. although   6. although

Page 63, Exercise C

Answers may vary. Possible answers include:

1. Unless Tabitha improves her computer skills, she won't get a job. Tabitha won't get a job unless she improves her computer skills.
2. Although Miranda does not take criticism well, she listened to Mrs. Addison.
   Although Miranda listened to Mrs. Addison, she did not take the criticism well.
3. Mr. Yeom is a good supervisor although he has a bad temper.
   Although he has a bad temper, Mr. Yeom is a good supervisor.
4. Cynthia will get to work on time unless she misses the bus.
   Unless Cynthia misses the bus, she will get to work on time.

Page 64, Exercise B

Longest: Air conditioning mechanic, maintenance plumber
Shortest: Vocational nurse

Page 65, Study Skill

1. 60 months
2. 36 months
3. $14.28
4. 18
5. High School Graduation or GED or Equivalent
6. Maintenance plumber
7. Maintenance plumber, firefighter, vocational nurse
8. Vocational nurse
9. Firefighter, maintenance plumber
10. Maintenance plumber

Page 66, Dictionary Skill

adapt:
    verbs: 1. adapt 2. adapting
      3. adapted
    nouns: 1. adaptation 2. adaptability
diverse:
    verbs: 1. diversify 2. diversified
      3. diversifies
    nouns: 1. diversification 2. diversity
    adjectives: diverse

Page 67, Exercise B

Answers will vary.

Page 68, Writing

Sentences that do not give good support and should be crossed out:

1. In both of those accidents, I fell asleep behind the wheel.
2. The hospital admitting staff has criticized my notes numerous times for bad handwriting, but I am working on this.
3. However, a month ago I administered CPR incorrectly to a woman and injured her.
4. I was tired from working overtime.
5. Several patients have complained that I did not answer their questions.

Page 69, Exercise A

1. c   2. d   3. b   4. a

Page 69, Exercise B

1. adjust   3. flexible
2. concentrate 4. factor

Page 69, Exercise C

Answers will vary.

UNIT 6

Page 70, Dictionary Skill

1. c   3. h   5. a   7. d
2. f   4. e   6. g   8. b

Page 71, Exercise A

1. manicure   5. octopus
2. manually   6. podiatrist
3. dental   7. digit
4. dentist   8. digital

Page 71, Exercise B

1. dentist   4. manicure
2. octopus   5. manually
3. podiatrist 6. digit

Page 72, Exercise A

Chlorpheniramine maleate

Page 72, Exercise B

1. T   3. F   5. T
2. F   4. F

Page 73, Study Skill

1. 6   3. 5   5. 10
2. 1   4. 1/2 6. 4

Page 74, Read

A. Choking
B. CPR
C. Bites

Page 75, Exercise A

1. e   2. c   3. a   4. b   5. d

Page 75, Exercise B

1. F   3. T   5. F   7. F
2. T   4. F   6. T   8. F

Page 75, Exercise C

1. You should put an antibiotic cream on a bite after you wash it.
4. You should not wait for a doctor to give first aid to a choking person.
5. Stand behind a person when doing the Heimlich maneuver.
7. In CPR, push on the chest before you give mouth-to-mouth breathing.
8. If you aren't trained in CPR, you can use the hand technique every two seconds until trained help arrives.

Page 76, Exercise A

1. Can you tell me what's wrong with Paul?
   I'm not sure what's wrong with Paul.
2. I wonder whether Beatriz will call 911.
3. Could you tell me if Mariam knows how to perform CPR?

Page 76, Exercise B

1. Do you know how Tao is feeling today?
2. I'm sure Alicia will go to the doctor this week.
3. I wonder why Anh is in shock.
4. Could you tell me if Mr. Duval needs insulin?
5. I don't know if you are giving the medicine correctly.

Page 77, Exercise C

Answers may vary. Possible answers:

1. Can/Could you tell me who Don's doctor is?
2. Can/Could you tell me what kind of surgery Mrs. Popova is having?
3. Can/Could you tell me where the first aid class is?
4. Can/Could you tell me why Yuan is calling 911?

Page 77, Exercise D

Answers may vary. Possible answers:

1. Could you tell me where Kate is
2. I don't know what's wrong with her
3. Could you tell me her phone number
4. I'm not sure how late the FlowerMart is open

Page 78, Read

breast cancer, cervical cancer, vaginal cancer, flu, heart disease, stroke, lung disease, Hepatitis B

Page 79, Exercise A

Signal words

1. The risk increases with age, so women over age forty need to get a yearly mammogram.
2. Women who have breast cancer in the family (a mother, sister) are at risk, so they should start having mammograms after age thirty-five.
3. Women of any age can get these cancers, so women twenty-one and over should get a pap test every year.
4. Influenza season is November to April, so flu shots are given at this time.
5. When people are sick with a cold, however, they should not get a flu shot because it can make them sicker.
6. Smoking can lead to many diseases . . .
7. Hepatitis B is spread through blood or fluids, so hospital workers should get shots for it.
8. Early prevention is important because it can stop people from getting sick.

Page 79, Exercise B

1. F   3. F   5. T
2. T   4. T   6. T

Page 79, Exercise C

1. c   2. b   3. c   4. a

Page 80, Exercise A

Sentences that give background information:

For example, many Americans eat one-third of the meals at fast-food restaurants.
Nutritionists say that most people should get about 750 calories at each meal.

Page 80, Exercise B

b

Page 81, Exercise A

1. e   3. b   5. d
2. a   4. c

Page 81, Exercise B

1. supplement   4. disease
2. treatment   5. records
3. pulse   6. symptom

Page 81, Exercise C

Answers will vary.

UNIT 7
Page 82, Exercise A

1. had established
2. had received
3. had made
4. had been
5. had started
6. had disappeared

Page 83, Exercise B

1. already
2. By that time,
3. By the time
4. already
5. already

Page 83, Exercise C

1. he had been a delegate to the First Continental Congress

2. no one else had signed it yet
3. he had already signed the U.S. constitution
4. Washington had already married Martha Custis
5. Washington, D.C. had not become the capital yet.

Page 84, Read

The First Amendment

Page 85, Exercise A

1. T   3. F   5. F
2. F   4. T   6. T

Page 85, Exercise B

Controversial:
something that causes a lot of disagreement between people because many people have strong opinions about it

Inappropriate Time, Place, or Manner:
Expressing yourself at the wrong time, in the wrong place, or in the wrong way (manner). This is not protected by the U.S. Constitution.

Page 86, Dictionary Skill

1. automate
   automatically
   automation
   automatic
2. colony
   colonial
3. justify
   justification
   justified
4. represent
   representation
   representative
5. restrict
   restriction

Page 87, Exercise A

1. unable, not able
2. unusual, not usual or typical
3. uncommon, not common
4. unjust, not just

Page 87, Exercise B

1. argument, a disagreement
2. enforcement, making people obey a rule or law
3. government, the group of people who govern a country
4. harassment, behavior that is threatening or offensive to others

Page 88, Read

b

Page 89, Exercise A

1. T   2. F   3. T   4. F

Page 89, Exercise B

1. the U.S. Constitution
2. Thomas Jefferson
3. 18 or older
4. Japan, Germany, and Italy

Page 90, Life Skills

1. F   2. T   3. F   4. T

Page 91, Study Skill

1. a   3. c   5. b   7. a
2. b   4. c   6. b

Page 92, Exercise A

A lot of people **walk** through this area, . . .
The East Side has a large number of empty buildings, and there **is** a lot of crime at night.
People **are** afraid of getting robbed
When you **are** in this area, you sometimes hear gunshots.
If the city **writes** a good proposal, . . .
We need to remove empty **houses** . . .
This **will** encourage more people to work and live in the East Side.

Page 92, Exercise B

1. problems: crime and garbage
2. solutions: rehabilitate the downtown area; remove empty houses or buildings; develop new buildings and hire more police

Page 93, Exercise A

1.	c	3.	e	5.	b
2.	f	4.	a	6.	d

Page 93, Exercise B

1.	federal	4.	automatically
2.	colony	5.	principles
3.	establish	6.	priority

UNIT 8

Page 94, Exercise A

1. If you are arrested for drunk driving, you will need to take a blood alcohol test.
2. If you do not have money for an attorney, the state will provide you with one.
3. If the police want to question you, they will first inform you of your legal rights.
4. If you answer questions from the police, your answers might be used against you in a court of law.
5. If you do not have an attorney with you, remember that you have the right to remain silent.

Page 94, Exercise B

1. If the court believes you do not have enough money for an attorney, the state will appoint one for you.
2. If someone commits a criminal offense, his or her fingerprints will be checked.
3. If you have a good lawyer, he or she can help you to tell your side of the story.
4. If you have been arrested you will be able to make one phone call.

Page 95, Exercise C

1. If he jaywalks, Joseph might get a fine.
2. If Robert and Jay trespass, Mr. Ramos might call the police.
3. If Carolina can't afford an attorney, Carolina's mother might pay her legal expenses.
4. If you are arrested, you can call an attorney.
5. If Mr. and Mrs. Novak call the police, the boys will be arrested.

Page 95, Exercise D

1. If he commits a crime, he might get arrested.
2. If you need to hire an attorney, it could be expensive.
3. If he trespasses, someone might call the police.
4. If the police stop her for drunk driving, she will have to take a breath alcohol test.
5. If she gets a DUI on her driving record, her insurance might go up.

Page 95, Exercise E

Answers will vary.

Page 96, Read

suffrage means the right to vote

Page 97, Exercise A

1.	T	2.	F	3.	F	4.	T	5.	T

Page 97, Exercise B

1.	F	2.	O	3.	F	4.	O

Page 97, Exercise C

1.	1920	3.	1913	5.	1917
2.	1870	4.	1916		

Page 98, Life Skills

1. verbal abuse
2. abuse of authority
3. abuse of authority
4. verbal abuse
5. behaviors/ actions

Page 99, Exercise A

1.	F	2.	T	3.	F	4.	T

Page 99, Exercise B

1.	T	2.	F	3.	T

Page 101, Exercise A

1.	F	3.	F	5.	T	7.	T
2.	T	4.	T	6.	T		

Page 101, Exercise B

1.	c	2.	b	3.	a

Page 102, Dictionary Skill

1.	I, F	3.	I, F	5.	F, I
2.	F, I	4.	F, I		

Page 103, Exercise A

verb: amend
noun: amendment
adjective: amended

verb: guide
noun: guide, guidance
adjective: guided

verb: murder
noun: murder, murderer
adjective: murderous, murdered

verb: reject
noun: rejection
adjective: rejected

verb: suspend
noun: suspension
adjective: suspended, suspenseful

Page 103, Exercise B

1.	amendment	4.	suspend
2.	reject	5.	murder
3.	guidance	6.	rejection

Page 104, Exercise A

And if you <u>don't</u> stop at a stop sign, and a police officer sees you, guess what you will <u>get</u>?

In both cities, if a driver <u>has</u> a moving violation . . .

It means that if you <u>get</u> a ticket for a moving violation, . . .

In Mexico City, if you accumulate twelve points, you <u>will lose</u> your license.

In Mexico City, if you <u>talk</u> on a hand-held cell phone while driving, you will get one point.

In Mexico City, if you drive in a bus lane, you can receive six penalty points.

Page 104, Exercise B

1. b   2. a

Page 105, Exercise A

1. d   3. a   5. c
2. f   4. b   6. e

Page 105, Exercise C

Answers will vary.

UNIT 9

Page 106, Life Skills

1. T   2. T   3. F   4. F   5. F

Page 107, Study Skill

1. b   2. a   3. c   4. a   5. b

Page 108, Read

d

Page 109, Check Your Understanding

1. F   3. F   5. T
2. T   4. F   6. T

Page 110, Dictionary Skill

1. countable   2. both

Page 111, Exercise A

1. greenhouse
2. public
3. solar
4. environmental
5. global

Page 111, Exercise B

1. global
2. solar
3. Greenhouse
4. environmental
5. public

Page 112, Exercise A

1. Silva wishes that she had taken a month to plan the event.
2. Ermias wishes he had brought in his glass bottles, too.
3. Nicole wishes she had come to the event.
4. Rafal wishes he had given his cell phone to his brother.
5. Rose wishes she had recycled the cups.

Page 112, Exercise B

1. had not taxed
2. had banned
3. had not blocked
4. had not banned
5. had not gotten rid of

Page 113, Exercise C

1. If Rita's co-workers had owned cars, she would have carpooled. Rita would have carpooled if her co-workers had owned cars.
2. If Mrs. Shi had known about the coupon, she would have recycled her batteries.
   Mrs. Shi would have recycled her batteries if she had known about the coupon.
3. If Yolanda had told Omar and Irma about the recycling center, they would have taken their bottles there. Omar and Irma would have taken their bottles to the recycling center if Yoland had told them about the recycling center.
4. If Mindy's clothes had fit her cousin, she would have given her clothes to her her.
   Mindy would have given her clothes to her cousin if they had fit her.
5. If Zhu had been aware of the price of gas, he wouldn't have driven so much.
   Zhu wouldn't have driven so much if he had been aware of the price of gas.

Page 114, Read

b

Page 115, Exercise A

a

Page 115, Exercise B

1. T   3. F   5. T
2. T   4. T   6. F

Page 115, Exercise C

1. a   2. b   3. b

Page 116, Exercise A

I have had it for a long time.
If I had realized how bad the gas mileage was, I might have told my brother to give the car to someone else.
About a month ago, I started looking at used cars online.
The salesman suggested a sedan.
He said sedans have much better gas mileage, and they are easier to park.
After I saw the ad, I looked up the trade-in value of my SUV.
I wish I had traded it in three years ago, when it was worth $14,000!

Page 116, Exercise B

six years ago
Back then,
About a month ago,
Last Friday,
After I saw the ad,

Page 117, Exercise A

1. d   3. f   5. c
2. a   4. b   6. e

Page 117, Exercise B

1. etymology
   [ORIGIN: 1300–1400 Latin *etymologia*, from Greek, frm *etymos* "true" + *-logia* "study"]
2. cosmos
   [ORIGIN: 1200–1300 Greek "order, universe"]
3. geology
   [ORIGIN: 1700–1800 Modern Latin *geologia*, from Greek *ge* "Earth" + *-logia* "study"]

UNIT 10

Page 118, Life Skills

1. Video deck, DVD player, Video camera
2. three
3. seven
4. one

Page 119, Study Skill

1. T   2. F   3. F   4. T   5. T

Page 120, Dictionary Skill

1. She collected **data** from many different places.
2. Manuel and Kim worked as **network** administrators for a large company.
3. (correct)
4. Our computers were not working because **the** network was down.
5. Her brother spends two hours a day surfing **the** Internet.

Page 121, Word Study

1. personal computer / I
2. local area network / A
3. compact disc / I
4. digital versatile disc / I
5. hazardous materials / A
6. virtual reality / I
7. public relations / I
8. National Aeronautics and Space Administration / A
9. as soon as possible / I
10. HyperText Markup Language/ I

Page 122, Read

to inform

Page 123, Exercise A

1. T   2. F   3. T   4. T   5. T

Page 123, Exercise B

1. a   2. b   3. c   4. a

Page 123, Exercise C

Answers will vary.

Page 124, Exercise A

1. Virtual reality is an environment that is produced by a computer.
2. Virtual reality is an idea that is very popular in films.
3. *The Matrix* is a famous film that is about virtual reality.
4. Virtual reality is a technology that is also used by health professionals.
5. Virtual reality shows ways that a surgeon should cut during surgery.

Page 124, Exercise B

1. that   5. that
2. who   6. which
3. that   7. who
4. that

Page 125, Exercise C

1. SkyTech is the game which uses simulation to teach basic airplane maneuvers.
2. Mr. Bui is the coach who uses virtual reality to help his students learn how to pitch a baseball.
3. *Biology of a Horse* is the exhibit which can be toured online.
4. *VisitMe* tours are the tours which are becoming more popular than traveling.
5. Computer programmers who work with simulators usually get paid a lot.
6. Athletes who use virtual reality programs often improve their game.

Page 125, Exercise D

Answers will vary.

Page 126, Read

YouTube's problems:

copyright violations
defamation / violations of its rules
age restriction / violations of its rules
censorship / blocking by foreign countries
limited revenue

Page 127, Exercise A

1. T   2. F   3. T   4. T   5. F

Page 127, Exercise B

1. 2005: YouTube was started.
2. March 2007: Viacom sued YouTube for $1 billion for copyright violation.
3. February 2008: Pakistan blocked YouTube for three days.

Page 127, Exercise C

Answers will vary.

Page 128, Writing

I grew up in a poor section of Sao Paulo, City, Brazil, that *was* called Cidade Tiradentes.
I spent an hour a day, *which* is the maximum time allowed a person . . .
I wanted to learn computer skills *that* would help me find a good job.
The telecenter also offered courses to people *who* had never used computers.
Six months later, I got a job as an administrative assistant to Sr. Suarez, *who* was the vice president of a large bank.
I went online and found a great website *that* described all the different neighborhoods in Los Angeles.
I think that the telecenter in Cidade Tiradentes gave me an advantage in life *that* helped me learn, grow, and move to new places.

Page 129, Exercise A

1. c   2. d   3. b   4. a

Page 129, Exercise B

1. engineer   3. innovation
2. data   4. criteria

Page 129, Exercise C

Answers will vary.